D0535286

COUNTRIES OF THE WORLD

Hungary

23472

WITHDRAWN

Gareth Stevens Publishing
A WORLD ALMANAC EDUCATION GROUP COMPANY

About the Author: Nicole Lundrigan has a master's degree in anthropology and a deep interest in different world cultures. Her knowledge of Hungary and the country's culture heightened after she met her husband, Hungarian-born Zoltán Deák. Today, she lives in Toronto and is the author of numerous children's books on culture and science.

PICTURE CREDITS
A.N.A. Press Agency: 75
Archive Photos: 15 (all)
Camera Press Ltd.: 74
Canadian Press: 81
Sue Cunningham: 10 (top), 17, 18 (bottom),
    19, 24, 27, 32, 66, 67, 71, 73
Karoly Dorabi, Sr.: 85
Focus Team Photo Agency: 3 (top),
    3 (bottom), 6, 7 (both), 16 (top), 22, 23,
    26, 35, 40, 41 (top), 47, 49, 50, 54, 55, 72
Getty Images/HultonArchive: 11,
    12 (bottom), 29, 31, 44, 59,
    60, 62, 65, 68, 69, 76, 77, 83
Bridget Gubbins: 21
Blaine Harrington: 16 (bottom), 41 (bottom),
    46, 48, 51
The Hutchison Library: 34
Interfoto MTI: 45
Björn Klingwall: 82
Minnesota Hungarians, Inc.: 84
MTI (Hungarian News Agency): 20, 39, 79
Newsmakers: 56, 57, 80
Pietro Scozzari: 42, 52, 78
Topham Picturepoint: 2, 3 (center), 4,
    9 (both), 10 (bottom), 12 (top), 13, 14,
    18 (top), 28, 33, 37, 43, 61, 63, 64, 70
Trip Photographic Library: cover, 1, 5, 8, 25,
    30, 36, 38, 53, 58, 91

Digital Scanning by Superskill Graphics Pte Ltd

Written by
NICOLE LUNDRIGAN

Edited by
SELINA KUO

Edited in the U.S. by
**PATRICIA LANTIER
MONICA RAUSCH**

Designed by
GEOSLYN LIM

Picture research by
SUSAN JANE MANUEL

First published in North America in 2002 by
Gareth Stevens Publishing
A World Almanac Education Group Company
330 West Olive Street, Suite 100
Milwaukee, Wisconsin 53212 USA

Please visit our web site at
www.garethstevens.com
For a free color catalog describing
Gareth Stevens' list of high-quality books
and multimedia programs, call
1-800-542-2595 (USA) or
1-800-461-9120 (CANADA).
Gareth Stevens Publishing's
Fax: (414) 332-3567.

All rights reserved. No parts of this book may be reproduced or utilized in any form or by any means electronic or mechanical, including photocopying, recording, or by an information storage and retrieval system, without permission from the copyright owner.

© **TIMES MEDIA PRIVATE LIMITED 2002**
Originated and designed by
Times Editions
An imprint of Times Media Private Limited
A member of the Times Publishing Group
Times Centre, 1 New Industrial Road
Singapore 536196
http://www.timesone.com.sg/te

Library of Congress Cataloging-in-Publication Data
Lundrigan, Nicole.
Hungary / by Nicole Lundrigan.
p. cm. — (Countries of the world)
Includes bibliographical references and index.
Summary: Provides an overview of the geography, history, government, language, art, and food of Hungary, exploring its customs and current issues.
ISBN 0-8368-2344-3 (lib. bdg.)
1. Hungary—Juvenile literature. [1. Hungary.] I. Title.
II. Countries of the world (Milwaukee, Wis.)
DB906.L86   2002
943.9—dc21   2001049223

Printed in Malaysia

1 2 3 4 5 6 7 8 9 06 05 04 03 02

Contents

AN OVERVIEW OF HUNGARY

Nicknamed the "crossroads of Europe," Hungary is located in central Europe and is landlocked, or completely surrounded by land. Hungary as a country first emerged in the late ninth century, when the Magyar people, a tribe of nomadic herdsmen who lived along the banks of the Don and Volga rivers in southwestern Russia, settled along the Danube River. Today, the nation is struggling to build an independent market economy after more than four decades of communism.

Throughout the country's history, Hungary has produced a number of outstanding scientists and classical composers, many of whom achieved international recognition. Hungarian folk arts are also among the finest in Europe.

Opposite: **The Fisherman's Bastion in Budapest is just one of the city's many historical buildings.**

Below: **Budapest is a breathtakingly beautiful city by day or by night.**

THE FLAG OF HUNGARY

Inspired by the French, who used the blue, white, and red tricolor during the French Revolution, the Hungarians developed their national tricolor during the revolts against the Hapsburgs of Austria between 1848 and 1849. The Hungarian flag consists of three horizontal bands of red, white, and green, which represent strength, faith, and hope, respectively. Until World War II, a coat of arms also appeared in the center of the flag. Although this version of the flag is no longer official, a large number of Hungarians still hoist flags that bear the coat of arms outside their homes on national holidays.

Geography

Located in the Carpathian Basin in central Europe, Hungary is bordered by Slovakia to the north, Ukraine to the northeast, Romania to the east, Serbia to the south, Croatia to the south and southwest, and Slovenia and Austria to the west. A modestly sized country, Hungary covers an area of 35,919 square miles (93,030 square kilometers) and has few hills or mountains. Mount Kékes, located in the Mátra Mountains, is the country's highest peak at 3,327 feet (1,014 meters).

Rivers and Lakes

The Danube River is a major river in Hungary as well as Europe's second-longest river, after the Volga in Russia. The Danube flows for a total of 1,727 miles (2,780 km) and cuts through many countries. In Hungary, the Danube measures 259 miles (417 km), and the Danube's largest tributary, Tisza, measures 354 miles (570 km). Lake Balaton is Hungary's largest lake and covers an area of 231 square miles (598 square km). Lake Balaton is a freshwater lake where Hungarians like to swim, fish, and sail.

BUDAPEST

Budapest is the capital city of Hungary and the country's largest city. It was formed by uniting three ancient towns — Buda, Óbuda, and Pest. Miskolc, in northeastern Hungary, is the country's second-largest city.
(*A Closer Look, page 46*)

THE DANUBE

Flowing for 1,727 miles (2,780 km), the Danube meanders through many countries, including Germany, Austria, Slovakia, Hungary, the former Yugoslavia, Bulgaria, and Romania.
(*A Closer Look, page 56*)

Left: **Parts of the Great Hungarian Plain are ideal for raising livestock, such as sheep.**

Opposite: **The Danube River floods twice a year, once in early spring and again in early summer.**

The Little and Great Hungarian Plains

Hungary is generally flat, with a series of low mountains that divide the country's land area into the Little Hungarian Plain, or the Little Alföld, and the Great Hungarian Plain, or the Great Alföld. The mountains, also known as the "backbone of Hungary," consist of various plateaus, volcanic peaks, and hills that are peppered along an arc. This arc extends from the Bakony Mountains to the Northern Mountains, which include the Mátra and the Bükk mountains. The Little Hungarian Plain lies to the northwest of the arc and the Great Hungarian Plain, or *Puszta* (POOS-taw), to the southeast.

Vast, arid grasslands once dominated the landscape of the Great Hungarian Plain, but many of them disappeared by the late 1800s when irrigation projects were implemented. Today, the country has about 100 square miles (259 square km) of Puszta near the Hortobágy National Park. The Hortobágy and Aggtelek National Parks are listed by the United Nations Educational, Scientific, and Cultural Organization (UNESCO) as World Natural Heritage Sites. The two sites have radically different landscapes and between them attract over two hundred species of migrating birds every year.

THE COWBOYS OF PUSZTA

Hungarian cowboys, or *csikósok* (CHEE-kohsh-ohk), have achieved an international reputation for legendary horsemanship. The cowboys of Puszta are famous for raising and training Nonius horses, a premium breed.

(A Closer Look, page 50)

Climate

Hungary has a temperate climate, much like other countries in central Europe. Hungarian winters are cold and moderately dry, while summers are pleasantly warm. The average temperature in winter ranges from 25° to 32° Fahrenheit (-4° to 0° Celsius), while the average temperature in summer ranges from 64° to 73° F (18° to 23° C). Weather conditions do not vary significantly from one region to another.

Rainfall is evenly distributed throughout Hungary. The country's low mountains and highlands receive an average of 24 to 31 inches (61 to 79 centimeters) of rain every year. The rest of the country has an average of 20 to 24 inches (51 to 61 cm) of rain. The driest parts of the country are the central and eastern parts of the Great Hungarian Plain, while the wettest region is in the southwestern part of the country.

Left: **Hungary sometimes experiences unusually cold winters, with temperatures as low as -29° F (-34° C), and scorching summers, with temperatures as high as 109° F (43° C).**

8

Plants and Animals

After enduring centuries of human exploitation, Hungarian soil has lost most of its natural vegetation. Today, approximately 60 percent of the country's land area is used for cultivation. Meadows and rough pasture cover about 22 percent of Hungarian land and forests about 18 percent. Located mostly in the Transdanubian region, the forests consist mainly of oak, lime, beech, and other deciduous trees.

Hungarian forests are also home to deer, wild pigs, foxes, rodents, hares, partridges, and pheasants. A wide variety of freshwater fish, such as pike and bream, live in Hungarian waters. Hungary is also ideal for bird-watching. Located about 24 miles (39 km) west of the city of Debrecen, the Hortobágy National Park has some of Europe's largest birds.

Near the border of Slovakia, the Aggtelek National Park in northeastern Hungary has a huge underground cave system and many limestone hills. Birds rarely seen in other parts of Hungary, such as the dipper, hazel grouse, Ural owl, and rock thrush, are often sighted here. The country's biodiversity, however, is suffering from increasing air and water pollution caused by industrialization.

Above: **Hungary's beech forests are dwindling quickly as a result of modern industrialization.**

Below: **Storks (below), crakes, herons, and ducks are native to Hungary and can be spotted throughout the country.**

History

Before the Magyars Arrived

The middle basin of the Danube, a region that extends from present-day central Romania to eastern Austria, was part of the Roman Empire for almost four centuries before the Romans lost control of the territory at the end of the fourth century. The ancient Roman territory was first taken by Germanic tribes and later by the Slavs. In the seventh and eighth centuries, the Avars, a nomadic people who migrated from the plains north of the Black Sea, dominated the basin. By 800, Frankish king Charlemagne had defeated the Avars and absorbed the territory into the Carolingian empire. The Carolingian dynasty controlled much of Europe until the late ninth century.

The House of Árpád and King Stephen I

In 892, Arnulf, Charlemagne's great-great-grandson and the last Carolingian emperor, called on the Magyars to help him defend his weakening empire from the expanding kingdom of Moravia (present-day eastern Czech Republic). The Magyars, at that time, were a federation of ten different tribes, and Árpád was the leader of the most powerful tribe. Led by Árpád, the Magyars conquered the land that became Hungary by 907.

ÁRPÁD'S JOURNEY

The Magyars' exodus from present-day southwestern Russia to the middle basin of the Danube has been recorded in history as one of the world's last great migrations. The origin and early history of the Magyars, however, is unclear, causing much debate among historians.
(A Closer Look, page 44)

Left: **The ancient Romans built the city of Aquincum where Budapest stands today. The Museum of Aquincum, the building behind the ruins of Aquincum, showcases artifacts recovered from the historical site.**

Left: This illustration is an artist's impression of the arrival of Árpád and the Magyar tribes at the middle basin of the Danube in the ninth century.

Árpád's great-grandson Géza I believed that Hungary needed to assimilate with the rest of western Europe to ensure the country's social, political, and economic progress. Géza's son Stephen I fulfilled his father's vision by implementing sweeping reforms to westernize the country's systems of government and law. He also converted Hungarians to Christianity and became the country's first king on Christmas Day in 1000.

The Mongolian and Turkish Occupations

The Mongols invaded Hungary in 1241. Although they occupied the country for only one year, the Mongols devastated the country and killed about half the Hungarian population.

The Hungarians restored their country slowly, taking more than a century to attain some of the highest standards of living known in Europe at that time. Hungarian civilization flourished, in particular, when King Matthias I (r. 1458–1490) was in power.

In 1526, the Ottoman Turks killed King Louis II and almost all the Hungarian soldiers that met them in a landmark battle at Mohács. After the crushing defeat, John Zápolya of Hungary and Ferdinand I of Austria both claimed the throne. Their power struggle further weakened Hungary and allowed the Turks to advance toward Buda with relative ease. The Turks took over the city in 1541, which effectively divided the country into three parts, each governed by a different ruler. The Turks were driven out of Hungary by 1686.

THE CROWN OF STEPHEN I

The crown of Stephen I is an important symbol for many Hungarians because it represents nationalism and unity. According to experts, the Hungarian Holy Crown is the only existing national relic in the world to have such a colorful history.
(A Closer Look, page 52)

HUNGARY IN THE SEVENTEENTH CENTURY

For most of the 1600s, Hungarian nobility ruled only the eastern third of the country, which included Translyvania (in present-day Romania). The Hapsburgs of Austria controlled the western third of the country, while the central region came under Turkish rule.

The Hapsburg Years (1699–1867)

Hungary was ruled by the Hapsburg empire of Austria after the Turks retreated, but the cruel dictatorship of Emperor Leopold I enraged the Hungarians, and by 1703, Ferenc Rákóczi II had gathered enough support for a rebellion. Eight years of bitter resistance finally ended with the signing of a peace treaty by the new Austrian king, Charles III. For about one hundred years, Hungarians made little cultural or material progress, and they did not resist the Hapsburg rulers. This period of relative peace was followed in the early nineteenth century by a national and cultural revival. On March 15, 1848, a revolt by a group of young Hungarian intellectuals led to a series of landmark reforms that supported the restoration of the Hungarian crown. The revolution gained momentum until 1849, when it was quashed by a Russian army that had been sent to answer the Austrian appeal for help.

The Dual Monarchy (1867–1918)

The Austro-Hungarian monarchy was established following failed attempts by the Austrian government to forcibly reabsorb Hungary throughout the 1850s. Losing two major battles, first to Italy in 1859 and then to Prussia (present-day northern Germany) in 1866, also made Austria less resistant to Hungary's quest for

ESTERHÁZY — HUNGARIAN ROYALTY

The Esterházy family of Hungary is notorious for its support of the Hapsburgs during the 1600s and 1700s. The family rose to power through a series of planned marriages, which resulted in a privileged status in Hungarian society and exceptional wealth. Despite supporting the Hapsburgs, the Esterházy family today is still regarded by many Hungarians as royalty, mainly because of the lavish lifestyle the family once maintained.

(A Closer Look, page 58)

Left: **Archduke Charles (1887–1922) went on to become the last Hapsburg ruler, Emperor Charles I of Austria.**

Left: **Many sections of Budapest were reduced to unrecognizable heaps of concrete and debris when the Soviets gained control of the city from the Germans in 1945.**

autonomy. Under the dual monarchy, the Hapsburg rulers granted the Hungarians full internal independence except in the areas of foreign affairs, defense, and finance.

The Two World Wars

Hungary fought on the side of the Germans in World War I. When the war ended, the Austro-Hungarian monarchy was dissolved, and the Treaty of Trianon was drawn up. Signed in Paris in 1920, the treaty reduced Hungarian territory by more than two-thirds, and the seized land was distributed among Hungary's neighbors, which included the former Yugoslavia, Romania, Italy, and the former Czechoslovakia. Over 60 percent of the Hungarian population became subjects of other countries.

The Hungarian government declared the country's neutrality in World War II, but the Germans occupied Hungary in 1944, forcing Hungary to fight against the Allies. When World War II ended, Hungary again lost some of its land area to meet postwar settlements. Hungary had to surrender any land that the country had reclaimed since 1938, as well as recompense several Allied countries for damages sustained as a result of the war.

THE TRAGEDY OF TRIANON

Throughout the 1920s, the Hungarian government, led by Prime Minister Count István Bethlen, strove to unify and rebuild what was left of the country after fulfilling the Treaty of Trianon. The contract indelibly marked Hungary's modern history and will continue to mold its future.

(A Closer Look, page 68)

13

The Communist Years and After

Shortly after World War II ended, Hungary held the country's first free elections in November 1945. Two of the six participating parties were communist, and they won not only a minority status but also a sizable number of government seats. With strong support from the former Soviet Union, the Hungarian communists reduced their opposition to two parties by 1947 and, in 1949, established Hungary as a people's republic under the leadership of Mátyás Rákosi. Hungary became a one-party state and adopted a Soviet-inspired constitution.

Hungarians resented communist rule, and on October 23, 1956, a revolution erupted in Budapest. The uprising was brutally quashed by Soviet troops, who also publicly executed many of the revolution's leaders. János Kádár formed a new government under the Soviets, and under his leadership, Hungary became the most liberal communist country in the Eastern Bloc. He followed a political course that agreed with Moscow's foreign policy but also improved Hungary's standard of living and internal policies.

FREEDOM FIGHTERS

Imre Nagy and his associates were key figures in the 1956 revolution that ended with nearly 200,000 civilians fleeing the country. Executed in 1958, the bodies of Nagy and his associates were reburied with honors on June 16, 1989.

(A Closer Look, page 62)

THE FALL OF COMMUNISM

Hungary's resistance to communism ended on October 23, 1989, and by the summer of 1991, the country was totally free of Soviet military presence. With democracy restored, Hungarians began the slow process of reorganizing their government and building a free-market economy. In 1999, Hungary became a member of the North Atlantic Treaty Organization (NATO).

Left: In a gesture both literal and symbolic, two soldiers in 1989 cut the barbed wire that once demarcated communist Hungary.

King Matthias Corvinus (1443–1490)

Matthias Corvinus, or Matthias I, was the younger son of General János Hunyadi, who successfully defended Hungary against repeated Turkish attacks in the 1440s. A kind and just ruler, Matthias I was not only a fine soldier but also a loyal patron of the arts and education. The land area of Hungary was at its largest during his reign, and he made the country a European center of politics, culture, and art. Bibliotheca Corvina, his personal library, housed many rare manuscripts, paintings, statues, and jewels that were admired throughout western Europe.

King Matthias Corvinus

Empress Maria Theresa (1717–1780)

Maria Theresa was the daughter of the Hapsburg king Charles III, who went on to become the Holy Roman Emperor Charles VI. With no male successor, Emperor Charles VI convinced the Hungarian government in 1723 to accept his imperial decree, the Pragmatic Sanction, which stated that Maria Theresa would inherit his original territories upon his death. In 1740, Maria Theresa became the first female ruler of Bohemia (in present-day Czech Republic), Austria, and Hungary. Despite her critics, she improved the living conditions of her subjects and provided Hungarians with forty years of peace.

Empress Maria Theresa

Lajos Kossuth (1802–1894)

Lajos Kossuth drew up the April Laws, which he urged the Hungarian Parliament to pass almost immediately after the bloodless revolution in 1848. The laws greatly reduced Hapsburg control over Hungary, and disgruntled Austrian nobles ordered a military invasion of Hungary. The impending violence spurred all of Kossuth's associates to resign. Kossuth became the country's governor and called for the Hungarians to defend their nation. Kossuth fled the country in 1849, when Hungarian forces were crushed after the Russian army intervened on the Austrian side. Under the guidance of Ferenc Deák, a legal expert and former associate of Kossuth's, the April Laws eventually became the constitutional foundation for the Austro-Hungarian monarchy.

Lajos Kossuth

Government and the Economy

The Promise of Democracy

Hungary is a parliamentary democracy. The post-communist constitution passed in 1988 by the National Assembly, which is the Hungarian parliament, guarantees democracy and multiparty representation. In 1989, one hundred amendments to the 1988 constitution were implemented to further protect the promise of free elections and a just government.

The National Assembly, or Országgyülés, has 386 seats, and each elected member serves a four-year term. The leader of the majority party in the Országgyülés is also the country's prime minister. The Országgyülés elects the country's president, who serves a five-year term. The president of the Supreme Court, the chief public prosecutor, as well as the Council of Ministers are selected by the Országgyülés, subject to the president's approval. All Hungarians over the age of eighteen are eligible to vote.

Above: **The Hungarian parliament building is impressively large and luxurious.**

Left: **The Hungarian parliament building is the largest parliament building in Europe. Located in Budapest, the building has ten courtyards, twenty-nine staircases, and nearly seven hundred rooms.**

Above: Hungary's military manpower base was about two million in 2000.

Local Government

Hungary has two levels of local government. The higher level consists of three sectors — county councils, which serve the rural areas; municipal county councils, which serve the urban areas; and the Metropolitan Council of Budapest, which serves the country's capital territory. County councils are split into village councils and municipal county councils into subordinate district councils. The Metropolitan Council of Budapest is similarly divided into subordinate metropolitan council authorities. The councils and their subordinate offices are responsible for education, health, and transportation. Hungary has nineteen county councils and twenty municipal county councils.

The Military

Under Hungarian law, all Hungarian males over the age of eighteen must serve approximately one year of military service. The duration of service depends on the section an individual joins. The Hungarian armed forces include an air force, a police force, a customs police force, border guards, and ground forces.

Economy

Hungary turned toward a free-market economy after the fall of communism in 1989. Since then, more than 85 percent of the country's economy has been privatized, and direct foreign investment in Hungarian firms reached U.S. $21 billion by 1999. The Hungarian government has also been trying to improve the country's economy with regional development and benefits for small- and medium-sized enterprises. Hungary is not an official member of the European Union (EU), but the country has maintained close ties with the organization since 1991.

Agriculture

Nourished by the Danube, Hungary's vast and fertile plains provide ample land for farming in the country. Agriculture, however, does not contribute significantly to the country's economy and accounts for 5 percent of the gross domestic product. Hungary is self-sufficient in terms of food and exports more agricultural and food products than it imports. Hungarian farmers raise cattle and poultry and grow a wide range of fruits and vegetables, including wheat, corn, rice, apples, and plums.

WINES OF HUNGARY

Tokaj is a small town in northern Hungary that is famous for producing fine wines. The villagers grow a special type of grape in their vineyards, which is used in the production of a type of wine called Aszú. Aszú enjoys a good reputation around the world.

(A Closer Look, page 72)

Left: Geese are among the various types of poultry raised by Hungarian farmers.

Mining

Hungary has large reserves of mercury, lead, uranium, and dolomite. The country also has the most bauxite in Europe. During the communist years, mining was an enormous priority, and the mining and metallurgy industries grew substantially as a result. They remain important components of the country's economy to this day.

Manufacturing

Hungary has a workforce of 4.2 million people. Almost 30 percent of the country's workers are employed in the manufacturing sector. Eighty-five percent of the country's exports consist of manufactured products, such as pharmaceuticals, construction materials, processed foods, paper, textiles, and automobiles.

Transportation

Trains used to be the most efficient and cost-effective way to distribute goods within the country, as well as internationally. The network of tracks, however, was poorly maintained throughout communist rule and fell into disrepair. In the 1990s, roads became the main way to distribute goods. Major funding from the Hungarian government has greatly improved the extent and condition of the country's highways.

TOURISM

Since the collapse of communism in Hungary, tourism has become a growing industry. The beauty of Lake Balaton and the historical significance of Budapest have proven to be great tourist attractions. Today, tourists, not goods, form the bulk of traffic on the Danube.

People and Lifestyle

Ethnicity

Hungary has a population of over 10 million people. Nearly 90 percent of the Hungarian population are descendants of the Magyar people. Romanies, or Gypsies, make up the largest minority group, at 4 percent of the country's population. Germans are the second-largest minority group, at 2.6 percent. Of the remaining groups, 2 percent are Serbs, 0.8 percent are Slovaks, and 0.7 percent are Romanians.

As a result of the country's tumultuous history, about five million ethnic Hungarians live in other countries, such as Romania, Slovakia, the former Yugoslavia, the former Soviet Union, Austria, the United States, and Canada. Also of Magyar descent, these people often describe themselves first as Hungarian, and then as citizens of the countries in which they live. Today, about two million Hungarians live in Romania, which hosts the largest number of ethnic Hungarians outside Hungary.

Below: **Hungarian couples today choose to have fewer children than their predecessors.**

Left: Hungarian Roma, or Romanies, often experience discrimination because of their ethnicity.

Romanies

Romanies form the largest minority group in Hungary. Culturally colorful and well known all over the world, the Romanies are often considered a wandering people. More than half of Hungary's Romanies, however, have permanent residences, usually in villages on the outskirts of cities.

According to the European Roma Rights Center, Hungarian Romanies, or Roma, experience a large amount of discrimination when they seek education or employment in the country. Some reports suggest Romany children are likely to receive their education separately from other Hungarian children, usually in separate classrooms and sometimes in separate schools. The center also estimates the rate of unemployment among Hungarian Roma to be between 60 and 80 percent for men and between 35 and 40 percent for women. The center believes Romanies are often refused jobs because of their ethnicity.

Discrimination of any kind is prohibited under the Hungarian constitution. In addition, many laws, such as the Employment Law (passed in 1991) and the Rights of National and Ethnic Minorities (passed in 1993), have clauses that specifically protect Roma. These laws, however, are not always applied.

ROMANY REFORM

In May 1999, renewed efforts by the Hungarian government to improve the Romany situation led to a series of measures designed to tackle discrimination in education, employment, health, and housing. These measures aim to develop a better antidiscrimination program for the Hungarian Roma.

Family Values

Families play an important role in Hungarian society. In the past, Hungarians and their extended families often lived together. Today, only a small number of extended families live together in rural areas of the country. A husband and wife and their unmarried children make up the modern Hungarian family.

The twists and turns in Hungarian history since World War I placed great pressure on the ties of previously large and close-knit Hungarian families. After the war, the traditional family unit tended to break down into individual nuclear families, but the families still resided close to one another. Family ties were further strained when the country came under Soviet rule. The extensive industrialization that followed forced many young Hungarians to abandon the family farm and work in factories situated far from home.

Modern Hungarians make special efforts to reunite with their extended families on special occasions, such as Christmas or Easter. Hungarians also see family vacations as valuable opportunities for family members to bond.

Above: **Most Hungarian couples choose to get married in church. In recent years, however, the country has seen a sharp increase in the number of divorces. Single-parent families are not unusual in Hungary today.**

Gender Relations

Men customarily head the Hungarian household. Before the country became communist, women stayed at home and fulfilled their traditional gender role as mothers and homemakers, while men worked on the land, and later, in the factories.

After democracy was restored in 1989, the vast majority of Hungarian women joined the workforce. Fueled by the need for more money to afford highly priced goods, even conservative peasant women in the country's remote villages earned wages as farmhands.

Modern Hungarian women often face the same dilemmas that trouble their counterparts in western Europe — how to prioritize their families and their careers. Working mothers are especially stressed by having to juggle a full-time job with homemaking. Many Hungarian working mothers spend a minimum of four hours every day on household chores in addition to working an eight-hour day. As a result, they have little time to spend in relaxing activities, such as pursuing a hobby, playing sports, or watching television.

Below: **Since the fall of communism, many Hungarian women, especially those living in the country's cities, have gained financial independence.**

Education

Before the communists came to power in 1947, the Hungarian educational system was controlled by the Roman Catholic Church. Most children attended elementary school, but only a small number of Hungarians could afford to send their children to secondary, or high, school. By 1948, however, the country's educational system officially came under the supervision of the state. During the Soviet years, every Hungarian was entitled to free education, but the communist government used the educational system to promote and instill communist theories and principles in young Hungarians.

Today, education is free and compulsory for Hungarian children between the ages of six and sixteen. Hungarian children attend elementary school, which lasts for eight years, between the ages of six and fourteen. Most Hungarian students enter secondary school in the year they turn fifteen and can choose to pursue their secondary school education in a college preparatory school, a technical school, or a school specializing in fine arts or music. Hungarian secondary school lasts for four

Below: **Children below the age of six are commonly enrolled in kindergartens by their parents. Hungary has one of the highest literacy rates in the world, at 99 percent. Slightly more men than women are able to read and write, at 99 and 98 percent, respectively.**

Left: **Eger University in northeastern Hungary is located near the world-famous Eger Cathedral.**

years. Almost every Hungarian town and village has a free public library. The country has more than nine thousand general libraries and about fifteen hundred specialized technical libraries.

Higher Education

Hungarian students usually begin their higher education in the year they turn nineteen. Higher education is free in Hungary, and some students are even provided with stipends, or allowances. The country has almost eighty institutions of higher education, nineteen of which are universities. The country's most prestigious and sought-after universities are in Budapest, including the Technical University of Budapest, Eötvös Loránd University of Sciences, Semmelweis University of Medical Sciences, and Budapest University of Economic Sciences.

Hungarian students have been increasingly enthusiastic about pursuing courses in fine arts and literature since the communist regime collapsed, but engineering and technical skills remain the more respected fields of study.

HUNGARIAN PHYSICISTS

Several Hungarian physicists in the twentieth century made remarkable contributions to the scientific world, including Leo Szilard, co-inventor of the atomic bomb.
(A Closer Look, page 64)

Religion

The Roman Catholic Church is highly influential in Hungary. Throughout history, the Church has influenced political decisions as well as shaped public opinion. In 1990, the Ministry of National Cultural Heritage (MNCH) passed an act that emphasized religious freedom, and the Roman Catholic Church was officially declared separate from the state. Today, the Church continues to play a prominent role not only in religion, but also in education and health care. More than half the population, at 67.5 percent, is Roman Catholic. Twenty percent is Calvinist Protestant, while 5 percent belongs to the Lutheran Church. Atheists and people belonging to other minority faiths, such as Judaism, make up the remaining 7.5 percent.

When the communist government was established, organized religion was discouraged, and those who attended Mass were subjected to much harassment. On prominent holidays, such as Christmas and Easter, when many Hungarians attended Mass, the communist army often disrupted the services by marching outside the church premises.

Above: **The intricately detailed interior of Eger Cathedral in the city of Eger is a breathtaking sight.**

Throughout the communist era, the government actively tried to improve its relations with the country's various religious institutions, but the Roman Catholic Church refused to retract its anticommunist stance. Protestant and Lutheran churches did not openly oppose communism and faced fewer difficulties because they were able to reach a compromise with the state. The government gave Protestant and Lutheran churches financial support as well as permission to hold services. In return, the Protestant and Lutheran clergies had to promise they would not interfere with the country's politics.

Judaism

The Jewish presence in Hungary dates back to the third century, when the country was part of the Roman Empire. Today, over 100,000 Jews live in the country, and they maintain a close-knit community. In the eyes of the Hungarian government, Jewish Hungarians are not considered an ethnic minority but a religious group.

Below: **Located in Budapest, the Dohány Street Synagogue is the largest synagogue in Europe and the second-largest in the world. Throughout the country's history, Jewish Hungarians have made significant contributions to the country's trade, industry, literature, and science. After World War II and the Holocaust, the number of Jewish Hungarians fell dramatically from 900,000 to 300,000.**

Language and Literature

A Unique Language

Hungarian is different from any other language spoken in Europe, and a great deal of uncertainty surrounds the exact origins of the language. Most experts, however, classify Hungarian as one of the Finno-Ugric group of languages, which are spoken mainly in northeastern Europe and western Siberia.

Spoken by over 98 percent of the population, the Hungarian language contains many unique vowel sounds and is generally unrecognizable to the English speaker. For example, *szálloda* (SAH-low-daw) is the word for "hotel" and *rendörség* (REN-duhr-shage) is the word for "police."

The Hungarian language has borrowed words from other languages, such as Slavic, Latin, and German. Early Hungarians also adopted many Turkish words. The Magyars adopted some Turkish words when they came into contact with various Turkish tribes en route to the middle basin of the Danube. More Turkish words were adopted during the 150-year Turkish occupation of the country.

Left: **Vendors throughout Hungary sell a wide variety of newspapers and magazines.**

Left: Hungarian author Arthur Koestler (1905–1983) was best known for his novel *Darkness at Noon* (1940). Many Hungarian works are translated into English today. Among them are *Rokonok*, or *Relations*, by Zsigmond Móricz; *A Pál utcai fiúk*, or *The Paul Street Boys*, by Ferenc Molnár; and *Szent Péter esernyõje*, or *Saint Peter's Umbrella*, by Kálmán Mikszáth.

Hungarian Literature

The earliest known piece of Hungarian writing is a eulogy that dates back to about 1200. In the thirteenth and fourteenth centuries, Hungarian literature consisted mainly of religious texts translated from Latin, such as the legends of Saint Margaret and Saint Francis of Assisi. In the fifteenth century, the Bible was translated into Hungarian for the first time.

Secular Hungarian literature flourished in the sixteenth century, when a significant number of nationalistic and dramatic works were produced. Prominent authors of this time included Benedek Komjáti, Gábor Pesti, and János Sylvester, who were also students of Erasmus, the famous Dutch philosopher. *Comoedia Balassi Menyhárt árultátásáról*, or *Comedy on the Treachery of Menyhárt Balassi* (1569), and *Tragoedia magyar nyelven*, or *Tragedy in Hungarian* (1558), were the two most acclaimed plays of that era.

The development of Hungarian literature slowed down between the seventeenth and twentieth centuries. The Turkish occupation, the Hapsburg years, the two World Wars, the German occupation, and the communist regime maintained a hostile political climate and a stifling creative environment for Hungarian writers.

Arts

Music

Franz Liszt (1811–1886) is probably the most well-known Hungarian composer of classical music. A talented pianist, Liszt composed *Ave Maria* and *Hungarian Rhapsody No. 2.*, which are still frequently heard today. Hungary was also home to illustrious twentieth-century composers, such as Béla Bartók (1881–1945) and Zoltán Kodály (1882-1967). Bartók wrote many memorable pieces for the piano and was himself an accomplished concert pianist. He dedicated much of his later years to preserving the folk music of Hungary and its neighbors. Bartók was struck by the unique melodies of this type of music and sought to immortalize them. These melodies were often passed from one generation to the next in rural areas and were not documented or written down. One of Kodály's achievements, like Bartók's, was preserving folk music, but, unlike Bartók, Kodály was interested only in Hungarian folk music.

BARTÓK'S WORK

First performed in Budapest in 1904, *Kossuth*, possibly Bartók's most famous work, was inspired by patriot Lajos Kossuth. Among Bartók's many piano compositions are *Sonatina for Piano* and *Piano Concerto No. 3.*

Below: The rhythms and melodies of Romany Gypsy, or Roma, music contributed greatly to the development of Hungarian folk music.

Left: **Members of the Hungarian Gypsy Company, seen here rehearsing before a performance at the Queen Elizabeth Hall in London, have been promoting the Csárdás internationally from as early as 1971.**

Dancing

The history of dance in Hungary is as long and rich as the country's political history. When the Magyars arrived, they brought with them dances that were mainly religious. Ancestor worship was a large part of the Magyar culture. The people believed frequent performances of such dances appeased the spirits of their dead ancestors. By the end of the tenth century, however, the Magyars' ancient dances were banned by the newly established Roman Catholic Church because they were considered pagan customs.

Italian dance steps and music heavily influenced Hungarian dances until the mid-sixteenth century, when the Ottoman Turks invaded the country. The victorious Turks allowed the Roma, a people of Indian origin, to enter the country. The Roma brought their unique brand of music and dance to the Hungarian culture. By the eighteenth century, when the Hapsburgs came to power, Hungarian dancing also had been influenced by German moves. The *Csárdás* (CHAHR-dahsh), Hungary's national dance, was developed in the nineteenth century. First performed in a village inn by peasants, the fast-paced dance tells a romantic story of love and heartbreak. Today, the Csárdás is performed mostly at weddings and other special occasions.

CSÁRDÁS — THE NATIONAL DANCE

In recent years, Hungarian teenagers have developed a renewed interest in the Csárdás. They first learn the original steps of the dance and then add their own spin to it, giving rise to many modern versions of the traditional dance.

(A Closer Look, page 54)

Embroidery

In Hungary, embroidery is not a craft practiced exclusively by women, as is the case in many other countries. Traditional Hungarian tailors and furriers, or people who make clothes from cloth or fur, respectively, take pride in decorating their products with intricate designs. Furriers tend to first make appliqués, which are then sewn onto the fur or leather garment. Tailors, on the other hand, embroider directly onto the coat, vest, or cloak, called a *szür* (SEE-ur). Hungarian women generally apply their embroidery to softer fabrics, such as linen and lightweight cotton, which are then used to make a variety of products, ranging from dresses to bedsheets to tablecloths.

Hungarian embroidery is characteristically done on linen, with a small- to medium-sized design that is tiled either throughout or along the edges of the fabric. The designs are usually floral, and colors that blend harmoniously are used to give the designs richness, texture, and depth.

The women of Mezõkövesd, in northeastern Hungary, are famous for covering the entire surface of fabric with intricate and colorful embroidery, while the women of Kalocsa, in the Great Alföld, prefer white, tiled patterns. The style of embroidery once popular in the 1600s and 1700s is enjoying a revival today in the city of Hódmezõvásárhely. Wool is used instead of thread, and favorite colors include pink, blue, brown, black, and green.

HALAS LACE

A product of Hungarian industriousness and ingenuity, *Halas* (HAW-lawsh) lace is treasured by collectors around the world. In 1902, when mass-produced lace was gaining popularity in Europe, a mother and her son from Kiskunhalas, a farming town in southern Hungary, invented a new way of making handmade lace. They sewed over paper patterns using only a needle and thread. The technique was unprecedented in the history of lace-making at that time, and their first efforts were well received. Halas lace grew in popularity throughout Europe until World War II. The Halas lace-making industry, however, did not recover fully from the devastation of the war.

HUNGARIAN PORCELAIN

Porcelain factories in Herend, southwest of Budapest; Zsolnay, a district in the city of Pécs in southern Hungary; and Hollóháza, in the northernmost tip of Hungary, are world famous for making exceptionally fine china.
(A Closer Look, page 66)

Left: This decorative tablecloth features traditional Hungarian lace and embroidery.

Architecture

Devastated and rebuilt many times over, Budapest has a rich architectural history. Today, sleek ultramodern buildings made of glass and metal stand in contrast to historical structures, such as Heroes' Square, three-hundred-year-old Turkish baths, and the ruins of the city of Aquincum. Built by the ancient Romans, Aquincum was a vast architectural project that included a town center, a military camp, and an amphitheater.

Budapest is also home to a unique architectural style called Hungarian art nouveau. At the beginning of the twentieth century, Hungarian architects borrowed heavily from local folk art and other Oriental designs when decorating both the interior and exterior of urban buildings. They created an architectural style that is at once modern and uniquely Hungarian. The Museum of Applied Arts, the former Post Office Savings Bank, or Posta Takarékpénztár, and the structures at the Municipal Zoological and Botanical Gardens are fine examples of Hungarian art nouveau buildings in Budapest.

Above: **Located near the Széchenyi, or Chain, Bridge in Budapest, the Gresham Palast, a Hungarian art nouveau building, has been turned into a casino.**

Leisure and Festivals

Leisure

Hungarians are sociable people who enjoy leisure activities that allow them to be surrounded by family and friends. In Hungary, two or more couples often go out together to have dinner at a restaurant or to go to the movies. More affluent, urban Hungarians tend to own holiday homes in the country's rural areas, where extended family members and friends are invited to spend relaxing weekends together. During these short vacations, adults are likely to head to the nearby vineyards for wine tasting sessions, while the children acquaint themselves with the country's more traditional way of life under the guidance of older family members. The children learn to start wood fires, cook using traditional utensils and ingredients, and embroider. During summer, Hungarians throughout the country love to take short walks in the evenings.

CHESS CHAMPIONS

Chess is a popular pastime in Hungary, and many people play the game well. The Polgár sisters — Zsuzsa (1969–), Zsofia (1974–), and Judit (1976–) — are especially gifted. Zsuzsa won the Budapest chess championship at the age of eleven and was ranked the world's best woman chess player at the age of fifteen. She went on to win three World Chess Olympiads (1988, 1990, and 1994). Her youngest sister, Judit, defeated Anatoly Karpov in a speed chess tournament in 1998 and became the first woman to beat a current world champion.

Left: Combining two favored pastimes, these older Hungarians play games of chess while soaking in spas or hot springs.

Lake Balaton

Hungarians live in a landlocked country and take every opportunity to be near or in water. Sixty miles (97 km) southwest of Budapest, Lake Balaton is the largest single body of water in Hungary. The area around the lake, extending about 19 miles (30 km) from the shore, has flourished over the years, with thousands of visitors, both local and foreign, supporting a variety of tourist-related businesses.

Lake Balaton and the surrounding area bustle with activity, especially on weekends. At the lake itself, visitors swim, fish, and sail in rented boats. Those who prefer to remain on land hike through the nearby woodlands or visit the regional museum, theater, or zoo. For the more adventurous, scramblers, or dirt bikes, can be rented to explore the natural landscape around the lake. Camping is also a popular choice for people who like to be close to nature.

Above: **Views of Lake Balaton are picturesque on a quiet day.**

WATERS THAT HEAL

Soaking in thermal baths, or naturally heated springs, is a popular Hungarian pastime. Many Hungarians enjoy visiting with friends while soaking in warm spring waters just as much as they like chatting over a warm drink at a café. Some baths, such as the Hévíz spa northwest of Lake Balaton, are believed to have healing properties. *(A Closer Look, page 70)*

Above: **Hungarian stadiums are never empty when the home team takes the field.**

Sports

Hungary boasts a strong sports history and has produced numerous Olympic gold medalists over the years. At the 1996 Olympics in Atlanta, Hungary won seven gold, four silver, and ten bronze medals. Swimmer Attila Czene not only won a gold medal for the men's 200-meter individual medley event but also set a new Olympic record. At the 2000 Olympics in Sydney, Hungary won eight gold medals for events in canoeing, fencing, gymnastics, swimming, and water polo, as well as six silver medals and three bronze medals. For a relatively small country with far fewer resources than many other countries, Hungary's athletic achievements are remarkable.

Hungarians are also intensely passionate about soccer and often fill stadiums to maximum capacity when their favorite local teams, such as Ferencváros and Kispest-Honvéd, are playing. Hungarians are very proud of their national soccer team and follow its participation in international competitions very closely.

Also known as the "Golden Team," the Hungarian national soccer team was a formidable force in the early 1950s. Led by Ferenc Puskás, who is often regarded as one of the greatest soccer players in history, the team remained undefeated for over thirty games. Puskás made his first international appearance in 1952, when he played for Hungary in the Olympic Games held in Helsinski, Finland. The team returned home with the gold medal. In the following year, Puskás' legendary left foot scored an even bigger victory, with Hungary becoming the first European team to beat England (6-3) at Wembley Stadium in London. The Golden Team's winning streak ended in the mid-1950s.

Tennis has been gaining popularity among young, affluent Hungarians in recent years. Players such as Monica Seles and Martina Hingis, both of Hungarian descent, have helped to promote the sport. Born in Vojvodina (a part of old Hungary that was annexed to the former Yugoslavia after World War I), Seles moved to the United States in 1986, turned professional in 1989, and won her first major title — the French Open — in 1990. Seles also won the bronze medal for the women's singles tennis event in the 2000 Olympics. Born to a Hungarian father and a Czech mother, Hingis moved to Switzerland when she was seven years old and turned professional at fourteen. In 1997, she was the youngest person to win a Grand Slam title in 110 years.

Left: **Monica Seles is about to seal her straight-sets (6-1 6-1) victory over Alexandra Fusai of France at the 1998 Wimbledon, or All-England, Championships.**

Religious Holidays

The influence of the Roman Catholic Church on Hungarian life is evident in the country's religious holidays, such as Saint Stephen's Day, Good Friday, Saint Nick's Day, and Christmas. Saint Stephen's Day (August 20) commemorates the religious accomplishment of King Stephen I of Árpád, who peacefully converted Hungarians to Christianity. Throughout the country, lavish religious processions are held in honor of the man who was declared a saint by the Roman Catholic Church in 1083.

Christmas is a special time for Hungarians. Preparations for the holiday begin on Saint Nick's Day (December 6). On the night of December 5, children customarily place their shoes near a window. Saint Nick, the Hungarian equivalent of Santa Claus, is believed to inspect the children's shoes when they are sleeping. If the shoes are clean, he fills them with chocolates and candy. If the shoes are dirty, they are stuffed with stones and twigs. On the morning of December 7, Hungarians begin to decorate their homes and businesses with Christmas ornaments, as well

FESTIVAL OF MOHÁCS

Mohács is a quiet riverside town in southern Hungary that comes alive with loud and festive celebrations once a year. Many legends claim to explain the origins of the festival, but to this day, experts are still unsure which version is accurate.

(*A Closer Look, page 60*)

Below: **These costumed dancers are performing for the people of Eger as part of the public celebrations for Saint Stephen's Day.**

Left: **Every year on March 15, Hungarians gather outside the Hungarian National Museum in Budapest to celebrate National Day.**

as prepare for the massive feast that takes place on Christmas Eve. Hungarians, however, do not decorate the Christmas tree until after dinner on Christmas Eve. Children usually go to another room while their parents decorate the tree with traditional felt decorations and chestnut candies wrapped in foil. Then the children open their gifts before attending midnight Mass with the family.

Secular Holidays

Secular holidays are also celebrated enthusiastically throughout the country. The most lavish secular holiday is National Day (March 15), which marks the first major uprising by Hungarians against foreign rule. On March 15, 1848, a group of young intellectuals started a bloodless revolution, and the fruits of their labor later became the foundation for Hungarian independence. Today, Hungarians regard National Day not only as a celebration of the country's freedom but also of the country's youth. Throughout the day, music and dancing fill Hungary's streets, which are often decorated with items bearing the national colors — red, white, and green.

THE HUNGARIAN ARTS FESTIVALS FEDERATION

Based in Budapest, the Hungarian Arts Festivals Federation has been organizing events that feature different aspects of Hungarian culture, including music, dance, folk art, and films, since 1990. These events are staged not only in Hungary but also in other parts of the world.

CELEBRATING THE END OF COMMUNISM

Since 1991, large-scale celebrations have been held in most major cities on June 30 every year. Even though this day is not an official holiday, it marks the departure of the last Soviet troops on June 30, 1991, and Hungary's subsequent move toward democracy.

Food

Hungarians have a deep love for food, and the country's rocky history has played a large part in the development of Hungarian cuisine today. Long periods of poverty brought on by war and political unrest led Hungarian women in the past to pride themselves on making inexpensive cuts of meat and simple staples, such as flour and potatoes, into delicious, hearty meals. Garlic and paprika, which is made from crushed and dried sweet peppers, are never far from any Hungarian kitchen, but animal fat, which used to flavor most Hungarian dishes, has since been replaced with healthier alternatives, such as olive or sunflower oil.

Breakfast is simple in Hungary. Most people have plain, fresh bread and a hot drink, usually hot chocolate for children and either tea or coffee for adults. Lunch invariably starts with a soup. Clear soups are prepared most frequently, but occasionally, an egg soup or a sour cherry soup is served. Dinner commonly consists of spicy sausages and cheese, which are eaten with crusty bread.

THE FEAST ON CHRISTMAS EVE

For many Hungarians, Christmas Eve is more important than Christmas Day because of the feast held on Christmas Eve. This feast usually includes several types of roasted meats, poppy seed noodles, sauerkraut soup, and *palacsinta* (PAW-law-chin-taw), or stuffed crepes.

Below: Paprika and garlic are so vital to Hungarian cooking that many businesses are able to make a healthy profit by selling just these two items.

Left: The basic recipe for goulash has been modified many times over the years to include different types of meats, spices, or vegetables.

Goulash is probably the most famous Hungarian dish. Originating from the herdsmen who lived on the Hungarian plains, traditional goulash consisted of small pieces of meat, onions, and a dash of paprika. Today, goulash also includes other vegetables, such as carrots and potatoes. Sweet peppers stuffed with spicy meat and a soup made of tomatoes and fish are other popular Hungarian dishes.

Dessert is an important part of any Hungarian meal. In Budapest, pastry shops displaying a vast range of sweets can be found on almost every street. The most famous Hungarian dessert is Dobos torte. First created in 1885 by pastry chef József Dobos, the dessert consists of six thin layers of sponge cake held together with creamy mocha filling and topped with a caramel glaze.

The Hungarian passion for food is evident during the celebration of special occasions, such as New Year's Day and Saint Stephen's Day. Hungarians believe mushrooms, pigs, horseshoes, and four-leaf clovers are symbols of good luck, and they try to reproduce them in edible forms on New Year's Day. A roasted suckling pig is usually served at lunch time, along with meringues in the shape of mushrooms. Marzipan horseshoes and chocolate four-leaf clovers are popular candies at this time of year.

COFFEEHOUSES

Coffee was first introduced to Hungary in the sixteenth century by the Ottoman Turks, who instilled a strong café culture in the country. This café culture has since experienced a series of highs and lows.
(A Closer Look, page 48)

A CLOSER LOOK AT HUNGARY

Led by Árpád, the Magyars trekked over 1,000 miles (1,609 km) to arrive at the middle basin of the Danube, or the Carpathian Basin. Their journey was so remarkable that some historians have identified it as one of the last great migrations. Hungarian history proved to be tumultuous in the centuries that followed, and the effects of the crushing Treaty of Trianon and the revolution of 1956 are still felt by Hungarians today. The rise of the Esterházy family in the seventeenth century and the centuries-long adventures of the crown of Stephen I remain topics of eternal debate.

Opposite: Jàk Chapel, an awesome example of Baroque church architecture, is located near Vajdahunyad Castle in Budapest.

Above: Vajdahunyad Castle is one of the most magnificent historical buildings in Hungary.

Hungarians are a warm and passionate people. These qualities are evident in their national dance, the fast-paced Csárdás, as well as in the boisterous celebrations of the Festival of Mohács. On the Great Alföld, Hungarian cowboys are still rooted in traditional ways and demonstrate their extraordinary horsemanship for thousands of tourists each year.

The birthplace of some outstanding physicists, Hungary is also the producer of world-famous Tokaj wines and fine Herend china. Divided by the Danube, Budapest today is a bustling and charming city packed with an unusually large number of cafés, museums, galleries, and hot springs, which reputedly have healing properties.

Árpád's Journey

Mysterious Beginnings

The arrival and subsequent settlement of the Magyar tribes in the eastern part of Hungary in the late ninth century may have established the first borders of the country. Many facts about these early migrants, however, continue to be shrouded in uncertainty. For example, the reason for their radical change in lifestyle from hunter-gatherers to nomadic herdsmen is a topic still widely debated today. Historians are equally undecided about how the Magyars' original native language developed into modern Hungarian, which is unique not only in Europe but also in the world. Experts in the past and in the field today have labored to find the missing pieces to this European puzzle.

Proposed by language experts, the most popular theory states that the similarities between the Magyar language and the Finno-Ugric languages indicate relations between the Magyars and other Finno-Ugrian peoples, such as Finns, Esthonians, Ostyaks, and Voguls. This theory suggests that the ancient homeland of the

Below: **This drawing of five Magyar soldiers in full ceremonial dress was imprinted from a carving etched in the sixteenth century.**

Left: **This colored illustration of the Magyar people is part of a Hungarian archival manuscript.**

Magyar people must be situated near the Ural Mountains in Russia, as is the case with other Finno-Ugrian peoples. Experts believe the Finns then broke away to settle near the Baltic Sea around 2000 B.C. The Magyars remained with other Ugrian peoples until around 500 B.C., when they began to migrate in a southwesterly direction toward the northern shore of the Caspian Sea, a landlocked body of water that lies north of Iran. The problem with this theory is that it does not explain what spurred the Magyars, who had been living in the forests with other Finno-Ugrian peoples as hunter-gatherers, to become nomadic herdsmen and then warriors. The whereabouts and actions of the Magyars until the early ninth century remain unexplained.

Árpád's Journey — The Last Leg

Many people regard the arrival of the Magyar people as the beginning of Hungarian history. Their arrival also marks the end of a remarkable 1,000-mile (1,609-km) journey by an incredibly resilient people. In 830, the Magyars arrived at the plain off the western bank of the Don River in Russia and settled there until 889, when the invading Pechenegs, a neighboring tribe, forced the Magyars to the western fringes of the plain. During this time, Carolingian emperor Arnulf offered the middle basin of the Danube to the Magyars in return for their help in defending his ailing empire. Around 896, Árpád, the leader of the Magyars, crossed the Carpathian Mountains into present-day Hungary.

WHAT DO THE TURKISH WORDS MEAN?

The presence of Turkish and Turkish-inspired words in the Hungarian language has caused much debate among historians. Some experts believe the Turkish words indicate that the Magyars crossed the Ural Mountains and eventually settled near the Don and Volga rivers in Russia. Here, they interacted with various Ural-Altaic peoples, such as the Huns and the Turkic-Bulgars, for many centuries. Other experts have suggested that Turkish words were adopted into the Hungarian language during the 150-year Ottoman occupation of the country. Alternatively, some experts have suggested that the Magyar people are of Turkish origin.

Budapest

Nicknamed "Paris of the East," Budapest offers spectacular views by day and by night. Formed in 1873, when three smaller towns — Buda, Pest, and Óbuda — were merged, Budapest is divided by the Danube, with the hilly regions of Buda to the river's west and the flatlands of Pest to the east. Approximately two million Hungarians live in the country's capital.

In the past, Pest was destroyed by the Mongols in the 1200s; the Ottoman Turks in the 1500s; and both the Germans and the Soviets in the mid-twentieth century. Each setback has required decades of rebuilding. Today, Pest is the economic, political, and financial center of the city, as well as the site of several pre-twentieth-century buildings.

Buda is the more historically preserved half of the city. Cherished buildings include Matthias Church and Buda Castle, which has been a World Heritage site since 1987. Also on the Buda

Below: **These cars are traveling from Buda into Pest on the Chain Bridge. Buda Castle (*left*) looks out over the Danube.**

Above: **The Hungarian National Gallery showcases not only some of the best work produced by local artists but also various historical artifacts.**

side, Clark Square commemorates Adam Clark, a Scot who built the first permanent bridge across the Danube. Made mostly of stone, Chain Bridge took ten years to build (1839–1849) and was designed by Englishman William Tierney Clark. Built in 1877, West Railway Station was a technical feat for its time. Constructed by the same people who built the Eiffel Tower in Paris, the station's hall and metal structures continue to fascinate thousands of visitors each year.

A Nation's Love for Fine Arts

The Hungarian National Gallery exhibits the works of the country's most distinguished artists, some of which date back to the tenth century. Gothic artifacts, such as wooden sculptures and altars, are among the gallery's most treasured items. The Hungarian Museum of Fine Art, on the other hand, features works of art by international artists. The museum showcases modern sculptures and paintings, as well as historical items showing Greco-Roman and Egyptian influences.

Coffeehouses

Coffee was first introduced to Hungary in the sixteenth century by the Ottoman Turks. Turkish coffeehouses spread quickly throughout the area that is now Budapest long before any appeared in Paris or Vienna. The Hungarian coffeehouse, or *kávéház* (KAH-vay-hahz), however, developed along the lines of Viennese coffeehouses, and the café lifestyle in Hungary peaked in the final decades of the Hapsburg empire. Budapest had approximately six hundred coffeehouses at the end of the nineteenth century. For decades, the kávéház has been a meeting place for people from different ethnic backgrounds and social classes. Today, Hungarians gather at a kávéház mostly to relax or unwind over a quiet drink after work.

Traditional Coffeehouses

The architecture of traditional Hungarian coffeehouses is unusually grand, and their interiors are plush. Establishments such as New York, Muvész, or Gerbeaud in Budapest cater mainly to tourists, while new, modern coffeehouses are the

Below: **In a Hungarian café, a *kávé* (KAH-vay) means one shot of espresso, with sugar and milk on the side. A *dupla* (DUE-plaw) refers to two shots of espresso. A large, milky coffee is a *tejeskávé* (TAY-esh-kah-vay).**

preferred choice of younger Hungarians. Traditional coffeehouses initially served only coffee and tobacco, but this menu soon expanded to include hot chocolate, desserts, and alcohol. *Eszpresszók* (ES-press-ohk) are usually smaller than standard Hungarian coffeehouses, and they also serve alcoholic drinks. Eszpresszók first appeared during the Great Depression in the 1930s, and many more opened throughout the 1960s. Budapest has the highest number of eszpresszók. *Cukrászdák* (TSU-crahs-dahk) are pastry shops that also serve coffee. Most cukrászdák are family businesses.

Above: When it opened in 1894, the New York kávéház had a lavish marble and bronze art nouveau interior and was visited by Hollywood stars, as well as royalty from around the world. The New York was turned into a sports shop for a while before reopening as Café Hungaria. Today, the establishment is again called the New York.

New Coffeehouses

The development of Hungary's free-market economy has led to a growing number of spacious designer cafés, such as the Odeon and Café Vian. These new establishments offer wider ranges of food and drinks than the traditional coffeehouses but are also a lot more expensive. Regulars at the new cafés are usually successful entrepreneurs, executives, or expatriates, who are more likely to chat on their mobile telephones than discuss politics or art.

The Cowboys of Puszta

The great Puszta, Hungary's vast grasslands in the Great Alföld, is home to csikósok, or Hungarian cowboys, who, despite the country's tumultuous past, have admirably kept their lifestyle and culture intact. Horses have long been a prominent part of Hungarian history and culture. In this picturesque region, large fields of paprika are dotted with modest, white houses, and the people living here appear almost untouched by modernization or outside influences. Women still wear traditional embroidered dresses similar to those worn by their predecessors, and csikósok manage herds of horses and cattle on the Puszta using only traditional tools and methods.

At an undefined point in Hungary's ancient history, the Magyar people, who were once hunter-gatherers, became herdsmen as well as warriors. A distinctive feature of the Magyar warriors was that they rode to war standing on the backs of their horses. The equestrian skill of the Magyar warriors, however, was not institutionalized until the 1500s, when King Matthias I came

Below: **The lifestyle of modern csikósok remains remarkably similar to that of their predecessors.**

Left: **Audiences from around the world continue to marvel at performances of the "Puszta five" or "five-in-hand."**

to power, and the Magyar men who possessed such fine horsemanship were given the name *huszár* (HOO-sahr). Some experts claim that *huszár* is a corruption of the Hungarian term for "twenty." This number is significant because King Matthias I built his formidable cavalry by summoning one male member from every twentieth house in settlements throughout Hungary to be schooled in traditional Magyar equestrian finesse. Consequently, the term *huszar* came to represent these legendary Magyar horsemen. Later, the English word *hussar* was used to describe fifteenth-century light cavalry.

The Puszta Five or the Five-in-Hand

Today, the "Puszta five" or the "five-in-hand" is possibly the most famous trick performed by csikósok. For this equestrian feat, five horses (three in front and two at the back) have to run in harmony. The horseman stands on the backs of two horses while holding the reins to all five horses. Csikósok are not only able to ride at swift speeds in this fashion but can also guide all five horses without losing their balance.

The Crown
of Stephen I

Two Crowns in One

A national treasure and relic, the Hungarian Holy Crown is actually made of two separate crowns. Shaped like a helmet, the upper part of the crown was originally a gift from Pope Sylvester II to Stephen I when the latter became king of Hungary in 1000. Made of solid gold, the upper part of the crown has Latin inscriptions and is decorated with pearls, jewels, and intricate enamel designs. Three gold chains extend from the rim of the crown, with jewels attached to each end. The design of the lower part of the crown is characteristic of Byzantine, or eastern Roman, crowns. The lower part of the crown, which has Greek inscriptions, was made in Constantinople (present-day Istanbul), the capital of eastern Rome, and was a gift from Byzantine emperor Michael VII to Hungarian king Géza I in the eleventh century. The two crowns were combined into one royal crown in the twelfth century.

Above: **Hungarians regard the Hungarian Holy Crown as a token of the pope's appreciation of Stephen's efforts to promote Roman Catholicism. The crown is also regarded as a symbol that marks the beginning of Hungary as an official state as well as the country's entry into Western civilization.**

The Long Chase

According to researchers at Mississippi State University, the Hungarian Holy Crown is the only existing national relic in the world to have such a colorful past. Hungarians throughout history have subjected the crown to some fantastic adventures to prevent it from falling into foreign hands. King Béla IV transferred the crown to the fortress of Klissa (present-day Croatia) in 1241 to safeguard it from the invading Mongols. King Matthias I brought the crown back to Hungarian soil in 1463, but it was hidden again when the Ottoman Turks invaded in 1526. Lajos Kossuth hid the crown in an iron chest, which he buried underground near Orsova (present-day Romania), after the country surrendered to the Hapsburgs in 1849. By 1945, the Hungarian crown was in the hands of the U.S. Army. The crown was kept in Fort Knox, Kentucky, until January 5, 1978, when U.S. secretary of state Cyrus Vance returned it to the Hungarian government. Today, the Hungarian Holy Crown is under the care of the Hungarian Parliament.

Opposite: **The elaborate and commanding statue of King Stephen I in Budapest is an appropriate token of the immense respect Hungarians have for the man who was later canonized.**

53

Csárdás — The National Dance

Nicknamed the "Tango of the East," the Csárdás is Hungary's national dance. A lively, fast-paced dance, the dance steps of the Csárdás were inspired by Hungarian folk dances, while the accompanying music drew heavily from the musical styles of the Roma people, or Gypsies. The earliest form of the Csárdás probably appeared in the sixteenth and seventeenth centuries, when the country came under Ottoman rule and was introduced to the lively songs and dances of the Indian-influenced Roma people. Early versions of the Csárdás, however, were largely left undeveloped until the nineteenth century.

Count Stephen Széchényi is regarded by many as the founding father of Hungary's national dance. During a ball held in the National Casino in 1839, Count Széchényi was dismayed by the fact that the night's entertainment did not include a uniquely Hungarian dance. He urged Hungarians at the ball to perform a

Left: **Both men and women wear intricately embroidered costumes to perform the Csárdás. To demonstrate their added skill and grace, women dancers balance containers filled with wine on their heads.**

Hungarian dance, but no one knew how. Baron George Orczy, a landowner from Gyöngyös, and his sister, Baroness Elise Orczy, finally came to the rescue with a dance they had seen the villagers of Gyöngyös perform.

By 1840, Hungarian folk dancing was gaining popularity partly because of the enthusiasm showed by members of the social elite, such as Counts Stephen Széchényi and Louis Forgách and Barons Stephen Orczy and Béla Wenckheim. In fact, it was Wenckheim who named the new Hungarian social dance the *Csárdás*. His rationale was that it resembled the dances performed in the *csárda* (CHAHR-daw), or village inn, by peasant girls on Sundays. Since then, the Csárdás has been well-received throughout the country by Hungarians from diverse social backgrounds. The upper classes welcomed the Csárdás because it gave them a sense of nationalistic pride. The common people were proud that the nobility appreciated and were willing to adopt a truly native Hungarian dance. The Hungarian Round Dance is the second-most popular dance in Hungary, after the Csárdás.

Above: **Csárdás music is characteristically lively and flamboyant. The instruments used to make Csárdás music include violins, clarinets, and bagpipes.**

The Danube

Flowing through more than eight countries — including Austria, Germany, Slovakia, Hungary, Bulgaria, Romania, Russia, and the former Yugoslavia — the Danube River is Europe's second-longest river. The Danube, however, is suffering from an ecological crisis. The river once had crystal-clear waters and provided Hungarians with a source of food. Today, its waters are cloudy and polluted from the indiscriminate actions of large corporations.

Between 1999 and 2000, the Danube contained dangerously high levels of cyanide, after a Romanian gold mine accidentally leaked large volumes of the lethal chemical into the river's water. The cyanide polluted both the Danube and the Tisza, and fishermen reportedly had to remove tons (metric tonnes) worth of dead fish from the rivers' surfaces and shores. For a long time, the Szamos, one of the Tisza's tributaries, smelled faintly of almonds — a sign of cyanide contamination.

Left: This fisherman holds up a fish that has been poisoned by cyanide. The gold mine accident has been dubbed the worst ecological nightmare to hit Eastern Europe since the explosion of a nuclear reactor at Chernobyl in the former Soviet Union in 1986.

Tests conducted by the World Health Organization after the cyanide crisis show that the Danube's waters also contain significant levels of other dangerous chemicals, such as cadmium and lead. Such extensive pollution raises a number of environmental problems, including endangering the wildlife that lives in and near the river, compromising the quality of farmlands once nourished by the river, and depriving thousands of people of clean, fresh water. Countries that were severely affected by the cyanide crisis, namely Romania, Hungary, and Serbia, have since come together to organize and implement major environmental cleanup programs.

Above: **The pollution of the Danube has had devastating effects on the inhabitants living near the river as well as the surrounding countryside. In Vienna, the International Commission for the Protection of the Danube River was established to address environmental issues regarding the river.**

The World Wide Fund for Nature

Hungarian waters are home to twenty-nine species of protected fish, nineteen of which reside in the Tisza River. Several protected species of fish are facing grim and uncertain futures. Since the cyanide crisis, however, the World Wide Fund for Nature (WWF) has volunteered to defend the Tisza's natural environment against further pollution and damage.

Esterházy —
Hungarian Royalty

Hungarians have mixed feelings about the Esterházy family. Beginning with Miklós Esterházy, an army officer, the Esterházy family grew in wealth and power by supporting the Austrians in the oppression of Hungarians in the seventeenth and eighteenth centuries. Hungarians resent the fact that the Esterházy family sided with the Austrians, but they also appreciate the significant contributions the family has made to Hungary's cultural life and fine arts. Pál, Miklós's son, was the first in the family to join the nobility. Pál was given the title of prince after he successfully crushed a nationwide uprising in Hungary, and, since then, the title has passed from one generation to the next.

The Esterházy Castle

Commissioned by Prince József, construction of the Esterházy Castle, or Esterháza, began in 1720. Located in Fertöd in northwestern Hungary, the castle reached the height of its opulent glory between 1768 and 1790. Empress Maria Theresa visited the Esterházy castle in 1773.

Below: **After years of painstaking restoration, the facade of the Esterházy Castle, or Esterháza, is as awe-inspiring as its interior.**

In 1681, Pál Esterházy purchased many valuable works of art that had earlier been confiscated by the Austrian government. The Esterházy collection of paintings and art treasures ultimately became the basis for the Budapest Museum of Fine Arts. Esterháza was also where the first two theaters in Hungary were built. Prince Miklós, Pál's son, was a fervent patron of the arts. He invited Franz Joseph Haydn (1732–1809) to Esterháza in 1762. Haydn stayed on as the in-house composer for over thirty years, composing and performing much of his life's work in Esterházy Castle.

In the mid-1950s, efforts were made to restore the castle, which had fallen into disrepair. Supervised by Professor Jenõ Rados, the Fertõd Building Cooperative was responsible for the castle's accurate and detailed restoration. Today, the castle receives over sixty thousand visitors every year. From June to September each year, classical music concerts are held in Esterháza's ceremonial hall. Distinguished local and foreign musicians play alongside symphonic and chamber orchestras. Staged by the Hungarian Baroque Entertainments, performances of classic operas and plays have also been revived at Esterháza.

Above: Classical music composer Franz Liszt was born in this house on the Esterházy estate, where Liszt's father worked as a steward.

PÉTER ESTERHÁZY (1950–)

Born in Budapest, Péter Esterházy is a member of the Esterházy dynasty and an accomplished author. He studied mathematics at the university level, but since the 1970s, he has won great praise for his stories, essays, and plays, which are often experimental and witty. His more recent works include *She Loves Me* (1995). Esterházy was awarded the prestigious Kossuth Prize in 1996.

Festival of Mohács

As tall men wearing sheepskin coats and horned wooden masks dance around a bonfire and fire noisy cannons, first-time spectators may think they are witnessing a religious ritual rather than a carnival. With many conflicting stories and legends, the exact origin of the Festival of Mohács, held at the end of February, is uncertain. Situated along the Danube, Mohács is a remote village in southern Hungary.

According to the most popular explanation, the aim of the festival is to frighten and chase away both the winter and evil spirits, which is why the men dress to look especially scary. Throughout the festival, villagers visit one another's homes in costumes and make a lot of noise wherever they go, using their voices, horns, or cattle bells. At the end of the festival, a straw effigy of the winter demon is set on fire, symbolizing the death of winter.

Below: **This illustration is an artist's impression of the Battle of Mohács in 1526, when the Hungarian army, led by King Louis II, was crushed by the Ottoman Turks. Mohács was also the site of the battle that led to the end of Turkish occupation. In 1687, an army led by Charles V of Lorraine defeated the Ottoman Turks at Mohács.**

Left: The precise area where the army of King Louis II was destroyed is believed to have been discovered about thirty years ago, when a mass grave between Pécs and Móhacs was uncovered. The grave contained the bones of over 280 soldiers. In 1976, on the 450th anniversary of the crushing defeat, a memorial park was established in honor of those who died. Hungarians, past and present, regard the soldiers who died as both Christian martyrs and defenders of the country's independence.

Another popular story says that the festival is a commemoration of a particular battle against the invading Ottoman Turks in the sixteenth century. Legend has it that the Turks were repeatedly unable to conquer a swampy area near Mohács because the villagers used a secret pathway that led them to safety whenever they were attacked. The Turks ultimately found the secret path and were advancing toward the area when the villagers, who did not have weapons, put on frightening costumes and masks and created a din with rattles and horns to scare away the superstitious Turks. The villagers' ploy worked so well that the Turkish soldiers dropped their weapons as they fled.

Today, the festival is celebrated in the form of a procession performed by three distinct groups. The first group consists of people who wear grotesque wooden masks, fur coats that have been turned inside out, and white trousers stuffed with straw. They also carry rattles and horns. Members of the second group wear fancy dresses but do not have masks. The third group consists of people who have covered their faces with ashes.

Freedom Fighters

Leading Up to That Fateful Day

Backed by the then mighty Soviet Union, Mátyás Rákosi became Hungary's prime minister in 1952. Soviet strength, however, weakened after Stalin's death in 1953, and several Eastern European nations, including Poland and the former Yugoslavia, took the opportunity to revolt against their communist oppressors. In July 1953, the Hungarian government replaced Rákosi with Imre Nagy, who lost no time in implementing reforms that steered Hungary's economy away from the Soviet model. The Moscow government eventually sacked Nagy in 1955 and reinstated Rákosi. By July 1956, however, Rákosi was dismissed by newly elected Soviet leader Nikita Khrushchev, who appointed Ernõ Gerõ, Rákosi's former deputy, as prime minister of communist Hungary.

Left: **During the 1956 revolution, Daniel Sego (*far left*) spits on the fallen head of the statue of Josef Stalin as a crowd gathers behind him. Sego was also the one who earlier severed the head.**

October 23, 1956

On October 23, 1956, a group of students marched through the streets of Budapest protesting Hungary's communist regime. The students presented a petition to the government, in which they demanded a formal acknowledgment of all the injustices the country and its people had endured since the government had become communist. The students were soon joined by civilians, who filled the streets to support their cause. Ernõ Gerõ responded with a condescending speech and later ordered the police to fire into the crowds.

Incensed by the senseless shootings, Hungarians throughout the country united in an attempt to overthrow the communist government. The Hungarian army not only joined the revolution, they even supplied the revolutionaries with weapons and ammunition. Prisoners who had been detained under communist laws were released, and Imre Nagy, a patriot well-loved by Hungarians, resumed his position as prime minister.

Hungary's liberalization lasted for all of twelve days. On November 4, Soviet troops swept into the country to suppress the uprising. János Kádár was then installed as prime minister.

Above: Singing the national anthem, Hungarians were permitted to hold a public commemoration of the 1956 uprising for the first time in 1989.

HEROES OF THE REVOLUTION

Nagy and his colleagues were eventually captured and executed. *Time* magazine collectively honored them with the title "Man of the Year" in 1956.

Hungarian Physicists

Leo Szilard (1898–1964)

Born in Budapest, Leo Szilard studied engineering at the Budapest Institute of Technology. A gifted student, he earned a doctorate in physics from the University of Berlin in 1922. In March 1933, Szilard moved to England, where he first worked on the concept of a neutron chain reaction. This theory later became the founding principle of nuclear energy and also led to the development of the hydrogen, or atomic, bomb. He continued his research in the United States but was deeply saddened by the use of his work in warfare despite his constant pleas to the government as well as the scientific community. In 1947, Szilard turned to biological research, which led him to invent the chemostat, an apparatus that is able to continuously produce bacteria under controlled conditions. Between 1959 and 1960, Szilard developed radiation therapy to combat cancer.

Below: **From 1926 to 1932, Szilard (*right*) worked with Albert Einstein to develop a prototype home refrigerator for Germany's General Electric Company AEG. The project, however, was abandoned with the start of the Great Depression.**

Left: Gathered at the opening of the Institute of Nuclear Studies at the University of Chicago were some of the American scientists who developed the atomic bomb, including Hungarian-American Edward Teller (*standing, first from left*). Upon arriving in the United States, Teller was enlisted to assist in the Manhattan Project, a division of the U.S. Army Corps of Engineers established in 1942 to produce the atomic bomb. At the end of World War II, however, Teller's research on the atomic bomb was brought to an end by a universally disapproving political climate. In 1950, President Harry Truman allowed atomic bomb testings to resume in view of Soviet progress in the field.

Edward Teller (1908–)

Also known as the father of the atomic bomb, Edward Teller was born in Budapest. Teller was a mathematical genius, but his interest in physics drove him to study nuclear energy. Teller, like Szilard, moved to the United States during World War II and was subsequently enlisted to assist in the Manhattan Project, a division of the U.S. Army Corps of Engineers established in 1942 to produce the atomic bomb.

John von Neumann (1903–1957)

John von Neumann made landmark discoveries in quantum physics, logic, and computer science. He studied chemistry at the University of Berlin and received a doctorate in mathematics from the University of Budapest. In 1930, he published *The Mathematical Foundations of Quantum Mechanics*, the most comprehensive book on the subject to this day. Neumann was a consultant to the U.S. defense forces during World War II, when he aided in the development of the atomic bomb by devising the implosion method, which causes nuclear fuel to explode.

Hungarian Porcelain

The intricate detailing and exquisite craftsmanship that goes into the production of Hungarian porcelain justifies its good reputation around the world. Herend, Zsolnay, and Hollóháza are Hungary's three most famous porcelain-producing regions.

Herend

The Herend Porcelain Manufactory is probably Hungary's oldest and most famous producer of fine china. Founded in 1826 by Vince Stingl, the factory is located in the small town of Herend, a short distance southwest of Budapest. In the nineteenth century, the factory catered mainly to the tastes of European aristocrats and nobility, producing elaborate dinner sets and complex display pieces. Stingl's products were of such high quality that by the 1850s, Herend porcelain was already being featured in world-class exhibitions held in major cities such as New York and Paris.

Below: Nicknamed "white gold," Herend porcelain is a mixture of kaolin, feldspar, and quartz. Kaolin is a white clay that makes the mixture easy to mold. Feldspar is what gives the porcelain a translucent quality after it is baked in high heat. Quartz makes the final product more resistant to cracks and chips.

Left: **This worker at the Herend Porcelain Manufactory is painstakingly decorating each piece of china by hand.**

Zsolnay

The history of Zsolnay porcelain dates back over two thousand years. The porcelain is produced in Pécs, a town in southern Hungary blessed with a pleasant Mediterranean climate. Zsolnay porcelain gained worldwide recognition at the 1878 Paris World Expo for fine china. Today, the finer works of Zsolnay can be seen in the Zsolnay Ceramics Museum.

Hollóháza

Surrounded by woodlands, Hollóháza is a remote village in the northernmost part of Hungary that became famous because of its porcelain factory. In its first ten years of production, the factory manufactured mainly ceramic tableware for everyday use. In 1954, the factory started to make porcelain and, since then, has manufactured only porcelain goods. In the 1980s, Endre Szász, a famous Hungarian artist, became Hollóháza's main designer. He made considerable changes to the design of its porcelain products.

PORCELAIN MUSEUMS

The Herend Porcelain Museum opened on June 20, 2000, and exhibits items that date back to the 1800s. The museum also organizes classes that teach the public how to distinguish between original Herend pieces and copies.

Operating on a national level, the Museum of the Art of Porcelain has more than eight thousand porcelain artifacts on display. The museum's prized possessions include a fruit basket decorated with 250 roses and the Herend cockerel.

The Tragedy of Trianon

Hungary after June 4, 1920

Many modern Hungarians are still suffering from the effects of the Treaty of Trianon, signed at the Trianon Palace at Versailles, France. At the end of World War I, the victorious countries came together to draft the demands of the treaty. Hungary was forced to give up almost 72 percent of the country's land area, which rendered nearly 64 percent of Hungary's population subjects of other countries overnight. When the Hungarian population was reduced from 18 million to 8 million, the country also lost approximately one-third of its Hungarian-speaking population.

The implications of Hungary's post-treaty boundaries further devastated the country by making it virtually inaccessible. Almost 74 percent of the country's roads, nearly 65 percent of its navigable waterways, and 62 percent of its railway tracks became controlled by neighboring countries. Most of the country's lucrative natural resources, including large reserves of salt, silver, coal, and iron were also lost after the treaty was enforced.

Below: **French soldiers salute as British prime minister David Lloyd George (*center*) departs from the Trianon Palace in 1919.**

Left: Trianon Palace in Versailles, France, opens out onto wide lawns and well-kept gardens. The Hungarians were party to the Treaty of Trianon, which was signed inside the palace on June 4, 1920.

Displaced Hungarians

As of June 4, 1920, millions of Hungarians suddenly became immigrants, even though they had not moved an inch. Today, as many as five million Hungarians proudly declare their ethnicity even though they live in other countries. Sizable Hungarian populations, ranging from five thousand in the Netherlands to two million in Romania, exist in over twenty countries, including Argentina, Australia, Austria, Belgium, Brazil, Canada, Czech Republic, France, Germany, Israel, Italy, Slovakia, South Africa, Sweden, Switzerland, Ukraine, the United Kingdom, the United States, and Uruguay.

The first generation of Hungarians to adopt new nationalities was generally subjected to harsh laws that sought to limit, if not eliminate altogether, many basic human rights. The plight of displaced Hungarians has improved over the years, if only slightly in some countries. Slovakia (previously northern Hungary) still bans the use of the Hungarian language in official places. The Hungarian national anthem is also illegal unless it is played to welcome an official Hungarian delegation that has been invited by the Slovakian government. In Romania, discrimination against ethnic Hungarians is widespread, especially in Transylvania, which was once part of Hungary.

Waters That Heal

Natural or man-made pools of warm Hungarian mineral water attract thousands of visitors to the country each year. Many people claim that soaking in these waters miraculously cures nagging ailments and illnesses. Hungarian spas and thermal springs are filled with water drawn from a variety of natural sources that possess differing mineral compositions and temperatures. Each type of Hungarian mineral water is reputedly unique and treats only one specific ailment or illness. For example, the water of Hajdúszoboszló is characteristically recommended for swift postsurgical healing. Dissenting experts, however, argue that Hungary's large reserves of warm mineral waters were used to heat homes and were not used for healing purposes in the past. Compared to the rest of the country, Budapest has the highest number of diverse mineral water pools.

HÉVÍZ IN TROUBLE

In recent years, the temperature and mineral composition of Héviz's waters have altered. A bauxite mine, located upstream from Héviz, depletes so much of the water supply that Héviz's fountainhead only works at half its optimum capacity, causing a gradual decrease in the temperature of Héviz's waters. Many believe that the lower temperature compromises Héviz's healing effect.

Left: Implementing a strict standard of modesty, the Ottoman Turks, who occupied Hungary in the 1500s and 1600s, erected separate spas for men and women. Turkish bathhouses in Hungary are still in operation today but are no longer gender-specific.

Hévíz

Hévíz, Europe's largest natural thermal spring, is situated in a valley northwest of Lake Balaton. The waters of Hévíz are slightly radioactive and appear blackish because of the mud that lines the bottom of the spring. Numerous lily pads float on Hévíz's surface. The earliest known record of Hévíz's curative properties dates back to 1730.

Famous Spas in Budapest

Gellért Spa and its accompanying hotel in Budapest's Kelenhegyi district are one of the city's major landmarks. The spa uses water that is rich in calcium- and magnesium-hydrocarbonates, sulfur, and chloride. Rudas Spa, in the Döbrentei district, was built in 1460 and uses water that is slightly radioactive and contains large amounts of calcium- and magnesium-hydrocarbonates, sulfur, and fluoride. Drawing water from the same sources is Rác Spa, in the Hadnagy district, which was once connected to the Royal Castle in the sixteenth century.

Above: **Gellért Spa has both outdoor pools and indoor baths. In Budapest, five-star hotels, such as Helia and Margitsziget, customarily employ in-house specialists who give the patrons proper medical examinations before prescribing specific bathing programs tailored to their individual needs.**

Wines of Hungary

Hungarian wines come in many types, including Eszencia, Aszú, and Szamorodni. These wines are mainly produced in seventeen regions throughout the country, centered around towns such as Tokaj, Eger, Sopron, Tapolca, Balatonfüred, and Nyíregyháza.

Famous Wine-Producing Regions

A hilly region in northeastern Hungary, Tokaj has been producing prized Hungarian wines, such as Tokaji Aszú and Tokaji Furmint, since the fifth century. Wine experts from around the world tend to classify Tokaji Aszú as an apéritif, or a pre-meal wine that helps to whet the drinker's appetite.

The old city of Eger lies between the Mátra Mountains and the northern reaches of the Tisza River. The city is mostly known for its many Baroque buildings, but it also has a tradition of producing fine wines, such as Bikavér, Egri Leányka, and Egri Medoc Noir. The most favored of Eger wines, Bikavér, which means "bull's blood," was so named because of its rich, red color.

Below: **Legend has it that the hilly landscape of Tokaj came into being after volcanic ash spewed by two volcanoes, in separate eruptions, had settled.**

Making Aszú and Eszencia

Grapes cultivated for the production of Aszú wine are left on the vine until they are attacked by fungus and shrivel into flavorful raisins. This technique is called the "noble rot." The harvested raisins are mixed with fresh grapes inside large casks. Then young village girls stomp on the mixture with bare feet until its consistency resembles that of dough. The thickened mixture is transferred to a clean container, where must, or grape juice, is added. Left to settle for several hours, the diluted mixture is then reduced to a liquid, which is portioned into barrels. The new wine is then left to ferment for several years.

The same type of grapes used to produce Aszú wine are also used to make Eszencia wine, and they are also subjected to the noble rot. Unlike Aszú, however, the harvested raisins are packed into special vats that each have a tiny hole at the bottom. The sheer weight of the raisins creates enough pressure to squeeze the juices out of the raisins. Drop by drop, the juices are painstakingly collected in a basin positioned underneath the tiny hole. The collected liquid is then bottled and stored for a minimum of twenty-five years.

Above: **Aszú and Eszencia are made from the same type of grapes. Eszencia, however, is more flavorful because it is not diluted by must.**

RELATIONS WITH NORTH AMERICA

Relations between Hungary and North America have not always been warm. From World War I until the fall of the Soviet Union in 1991, negative relations existed between Hungary and North America because of conflicting political decisions and ideas. Tension between Hungary and the United States reached its height when Hungarians were behind the iron curtain. Not only were the two countries already at odds over their opposing systems of government, Hungarians were also resentful that their beloved national artifact — the Hungarian Holy Crown — was held by the United States.

Opposite: **President Bill Clinton (***third from right***) received Hungarian president Árpad Goncz (***right***) at the White House in June 1999.**

North America, however, remained sympathetic to Hungarian civilians during those troubled years and accepted scores of political refugees. Today, the United States and Canada are home to nearly 900,000 Hungarians. The United States eventually returned the crown in 1978, and the gesture marked the beginning of a fruitful friendship. North America has given immense financial support to Hungary since 1989, when the latter shifted to a free economy. Today, the country is a member of the North Atlantic Treaty Organization (NATO) and maintains close ties with the European Union (EU).

Above: **Big American businesses have crept into even the less developed parts of Hungary.**

Historical Relations with North America

Hungary's political convictions have caused numerous points of contact between the country and the United States. After the 1848 revolution, Hungary was under the rule of Austria, which led Hungary against the Allies (including the United States, Great Britain, and France) in World War I (1914–1918). North America experienced its first wave of Hungarian immigrants after the signing of the Treaty of Trianon. Many moved to escape the harsh living conditions that came with being new citizens of Hungary's neighboring countries.

Hungary declared neutrality in World War II but was forced to support Germany after the Germans seized control of the country. Many Hungarians did not like German rule and fled to North America. Among this second wave of Hungarian immigrants were some of Hungary's most brilliant scientists, who later developed the atomic bomb for the U.S. defense forces.

Hungary's entry into the Warsaw Pact (which also included, among other countries, the Soviet Union and East Germany) after World War II worsened the country's relations with the United States. In view of the 1956 revolution, which brought about

Below: **In a bid to escape political strife, Empress Zita (*center, front*) of the Austro-Hungarian monarchy and her children, Prince Felix (*right*) and Princess Margaret (*left, back*), moved to the United States in 1940.**

Left: **Made in 1929, the Samuel Goldwyn film *This Is Heaven* explores the experiences of a Hungarian immigrant in the United States.**

democratic reforms, however, the U.S. government agreed to support Hungarians in their quest to overthrow the communist government. The support did not arrive. The U.S. government had diverted its attention to appeasing conflicts that had suddenly emerged in the Middle East. During this time, the United States received the third wave of Hungarian political refugees, which included numerous athletes, scientists, and entertainers.

Among the third wave of emigrants, approximately thirty-seven thousand Hungarians emigrated to Canada. The number of Hungarians emigrating to Canada has been nominal since 1957, with only a few hundred arriving each year. Today, four out of five Hungarians live in urban parts of Canada, and the vast majority live in Toronto. When the 1956 revolution erupted in Hungary, Canadians responded with tremendous support. The Hungarian Canadian Relief Fund in Toronto was immediately established to administer the collection of blood and monetary donations for an emergency blood bank. Within two weeks, three thousand eager Canadian volunteers, more than half of whom were not of Hungarian descent, formed the Legion for Freedom, an international brigade, to aid Hungary.

Modern Relations with North America

North America and Hungary have established strong ties in recent years that are based mostly on trade and investment. When Hungary emerged from communist rule in 1989, the country's economy wavered because it had previously relied heavily on Soviet-controlled industries. To help Hungary's shift to a free-market economy, the country received immense foreign investment, mainly from the United States, Germany, and Austria.

In 1991, the United States was responsible for 50 percent of all direct foreign investments in Hungary, which amounted to approximately U.S. $1 billion. By 1993, direct foreign investments from the United States had more than tripled to U.S. $3.1 billion. Trade between the two countries also flourished in 1993, with the United States exporting goods worth over U.S. $420 million to Hungary and importing Hungarian goods amounting to more than U.S. $340 million. Hungary's economy is slowly gaining strength, a fact that is reflected in the country's capacity to import more goods from the United States. In 1999, Hungary's imports from the United States totaled $968 million, and the country exported $1.3 billion worth of goods to the United States.

THE U.S.-EASTERN HUNGARY PARTNERSHIP FOUNDATION

The U.S.-Eastern Hungary Partnership Foundation (US-EHP) was founded in 2000 by the American Chamber of Commerce in Hungary. Aiming to promote and improve economic, cultural, and commercial relations between the United States and eastern Hungary, US-EHP receives support from both Hungary and the United States.

Left: **Apart from direct foreign investments from the United States, the U.S. government also provided almost U.S. $150 million in financial assistance to Hungary by 1993.**

The U.S. Embassy in Hungary

Located in Budapest, the U.S. Embassy keeps North Americans based in Hungary informed on current affairs in the United States. The embassy also provides consular advice, business-related information, and helps Hungarians who want to study in the United States.

Above: **Large North American corporations, such as PepsiCo and Ford, have factories in Hungary.**

Facilitating Trade

The Hungarian American Chamber of Commerce U.S.A. (HACCUSA) was founded in 1992 by Monika Szarka Elling, president and chief executive officer of Global Advisory Networks. Through HACCUSA, she extensively marketed Hungary to potential investors in the United States and improved diplomatic relations between the two countries. Elling has presented at the White House Conference in Cleveland, the Global Trade 2000 Conference, and Trade 2000 Hungary-U.S. She also works closely with the commercial section of the U.S. Embassy in Hungary, as well as the U.S. Department of Commerce in Washington, D.C.

Hungarians in the United States

In the past, political refugees made up the bulk of Hungarian immigrants to the United States. Today, approximately 730,000 Hungarians reside in the United States, and significant Hungarian populations exist in most major cities, especially in the eastern states of New York, Connecticut, and New Jersey. Hungarian-Americans are proud of their heritage and are passionate about maintaining the spirit of Hungarian culture in their new homelands. Nearly every city and suburb with a sizable Hungarian population has a Hungarian hall, where Hungarians meet and exchange news and information from home. Several balls are also held each year to celebrate Hungarian culture, such as the Hunter's Ball, which is held in December, and Sylvester's Ball, which is held on New Year's Eve.

Organized by Hungarians Abroad, a two-day conference, *Hungarians in the Media — Hungarian Media Strategy*, was held in Budapest in April 2000. The conference was attended by over eighty prominent Hungarians from all over the world, three of whom were members of the Hungarian American Coalition based in Washington, D.C. The coalition's focus at the conference was how to achieve accurate representations of Hungary and Hungarians in the American media.

THE YOUNGEST CONSUL-GENERAL

Hungarian-American Dr. László Molnár is the youngest person to assume the position of ambassador at the New York consulate in New York City. About 150,000 Hungarians live in Manhattan, but the city does not have an official center for Hungarian arts and culture. Molnár is working on establishing one and hopes that second and third generation Hungarians will support the center.

Below: Special members of the Hungarian police force are trained at the Federal Bureau of Investigation (FBI).

Left: **Tamas Buday, Jr., (*front, right*) greets Hungarian paddler Csaba Horvath (*front, left*) after the Hungarian team won the silver medal in the C-2 1000-meter event at the world canoe championships held in Dartmouth, Nova Scotia, on August 23, 1997. Both Tamas Buday and his brother, Attila, (*behind right*) are Canadians of Hungarian descent.**

Hungarians in Canada

Today, about 140,000 Hungarians live in Canada. Most Hungarian-Canadians live in Toronto. Stephen Parmenius, who worked for English explorer Sir Humphrey Gilbert, was the first known Hungarian to arrive in Canada in 1583. Recorded in his diary were some of the earliest impressions Europeans had of Newfoundland. Hungarians arrived in Canada in large numbers about three hundred years later. Among the first wave of Hungarian emigrants to North America, 2 percent settled in Canada, while the bulk settled in the United States. Between 1925 and 1930, Canada received approximately twenty-six thousand Hungarian immigrants. Unlike the first wave of Hungarians, who settled in the remote Canadian prairies, the second wave of immigrants settled in major Canadian cities. The third wave of Hungarian emigration occurred after World War II. In the years immediately following the war, twelve thousand Hungarians emigrated to Canada because some had lost everything to the Germans, while others feared what the Soviet occupation would do to their lifestyles. Unlike the previous waves of immigration, these Hungarians were middle or upper-middle class people who were well-educated and held good jobs.

North Americans in Hungary

Tourists make up the bulk of North Americans in Hungary. Although a significant number of Americans are exchange students, the majority of North Americans living in the country are businesspeople.

In 1999, profits from the tourist industry soared, and North American visitors contributed much of that revenue. Tourism has boomed in Hungary since the collapse of communism. North American visitors are drawn by Hungary's historical cities, thermal springs, and unique culture.

Ecotourism is also on the rise in Hungary. With so many untouched waterways, North Americans are flocking to the country to water raft and canoe. Hiking trips are becoming popular as well, with tourists trekking through the forests and grasslands around Lake Balaton to view flora and fauna that are unique to the region. Hungary also boasts a large number of national parks that are open to the public.

STUDENT EXCHANGE PROGRAMS

The College of Liberal Arts at the University of New Hampshire has a study abroad program in Budapest. The program gives American students a chance to experience European culture while completing their course work for the semester. Kossuth University is also actively establishing ties with universities from the United States and Canada, including Rutgers and the State University of New Jersey. The Technical University of Budapest has affiliations with Florida State University. Before these ties were established, Hungarian students were usually sent on exchanges via international programs, such as Tempus or the International Student Exchange Program (ISEP).

Left: Popular American plays and Broadway musicals, such as *West Side Story*, are now performed at theaters throughout Hungary's major cities.

Left: Zsa Zsa Gabor (*left*) and her sisters were among the earliest Hungarians to become famous in the United States. Zsa Zsa starred in a number of Hollywood films.

Famous Hungarians in North America

Many famous Americans are of Hungarian descent, especially in the fields of entertainment and science and technology. Hungarian-born Adolph Zukor (1873–1976) was the founder of Paramount Pictures. He also produced the first full-length feature film — *The Prisoner of Zenda* (1937) — in the United States. Also born in Hungary, Andrew Vajna, an accomplished producer, created many blockbusters throughout his illustrious career, including the *Rambo* films (1982, 1985, 1988), *Die Hard* (1988), *Total Recall* (1990), *Nixon* (1995), and *Evita* (1996). The Academy Award winning director of *My Fair Lady* (1964), George Cukor, is also of Hungarian descent. Born Vilmos Friedman, William Fox was the founder of Fox Company, which merged with Twentieth Century Pictures in 1935 to become Twentieth Century Fox.

In the field of science and technology, Hungarian-Americans have made some truly remarkable contributions. Apart from the brilliant Hungarian scientists who invented the atomic bomb, Andy Grove, chairman and co-founder of Intel, also won *Time* magazine's "1998 Man of the Year" award for his achievements in computer technology.

JOSEPH PULITZER (1847–1911)

Hungarian-born American Joseph Pulitzer arrived in the United States at the age of seventeen. Rising quickly, he started as a reporter and became editor and co-owner of a newspaper after four years. Pulitzer left the newspaper to start a career in politics. Although he was well received as a politician, Pulitzer's passion for news still burned. He purchased *World*, a daily newspaper in New York, after completing a law degree and went on to expose political scandals and corrupt businesses. Pulitzer fully supported unions and the working class. He also contributed toward the building costs of the Statue of Liberty. Pulitzer left U.S. $1 million in his will to Columbia University to build a journalism school and established the Pulitzer Prize. Today, the prize is awarded only to people who have achieved the highest standards of journalism.

Hungarian Influence in North America

Hungarian immigrants in the past may have assimilated quite well into North American society over the years. Many, however, still seek to protect their cultural identity by establishing Hungarian associations, restaurants, bakeries, and bookshops.

Many North American universities have Hungarian student associations. The Hungarian Student Association at the University of Toronto is where Hungarian students who are new to Canada can get to know their host country better by meeting and chatting with local students, who, in turn, can also acquaint themselves with aspects of Hungarian culture. The aim of the American Hungarian Heritage Association in Stratford, Connecticut, is to preserve and promote any form of Hungarian culture in the United States.

Hungarian flavors have found their way into North American food. Goulash, for example, is served in many non-Hungarian restaurants in North America, and Hungarian food, such as spicy sausage and bacon biscuits, is sold in many North American supermarkets.

Below: **These Hungarian-Americans are members of Minnesota Hungarians, Inc., a nonprofit organization set up for Minnesotans of Hungarian descent. The association aims to preserve, protect, and promote Hungarian culture in the United States.**

Reflecting the significant number of homesick Hungarians who once lived in the area, Yorkville, Manhattan, once had several Hungarian restaurants, including Csárdá, Red Tulip, and Mocca. Today, Mocca is the only Hungarian eatery left. In the same area, Paprika Weiss was a Hungarian shop that sold nothing but paprika in a myriad of varieties before it was converted into a diner.

Based in Cleveland, the Csárdás Dance Company is dedicated to preserving Hungarian songs, dances, and music. The company has Hungarian and non-Hungarian members, who frequently perform traditional Hungarian folk dances as well as modern dances inspired by traditional forms. The company's efforts were rewarded when their performances in Budapest earned praise from local critics for their authenticity.

The aim of the Ottawa Hungarian Folkdance Chamber Group is to preserve and document folk culture from various parts of Hungary. The group is especially interested in folk costumes, arts and crafts, and the Csárdás.

Above: **The Hungarian Folkdance Chamber Group of Ottawa was founded in 1987.**

HUNGARIAN FILMS IN NORTH AMERICA

Modern Hungarian filmmakers are gaining respect in North America, and István Szabo leads the way. His film *Sunshine* is an epic about the pain and suffering endured by several generations of Hungarian Jews. The film gave North Americans insight into the troubled history of Hungary as well as a taste of daily life in Hungary.

A B C D

1

CZECH
REPUBLIC

SLOVAKIA

Carpathia

Aggtelek
National Park

2

Danube

AUSTRIA

NÓGRÁD
Northern Mour
Mount Kékes
(3,327ft/1,014m)▲
Mátra Mountains

Gyöngy

GYÕR-MOSON-
SOPRON

Sopron

Fertõd

KOMÁROM-
ESZTERGOM

BUDAPEST

BUDAPEST

LITTLE ALFÖLD

N

3

VAS

VESZPRÉM

FEJÉR

PEST

JÁ
NAG
SZO

Herend

Bakony Mountains

Danube

Tapolca

Balatonfüred

Hévíz

Lake
Balaton

BÁCS-KISKUN

GREAT ALF

ZALA

SOMOGY

TOLNA

SLOVENIA

TRANSDANUBIA

Kalocsa

Kiskunhalas

CSONG

Hódmezõvásá

Szeged

4

Pécs

Mohács

BARANYA

CROATIA

SERBIA

5

Danube

HUNGARY

E　　　**F**

o　u　n　t　a　i　n　s

Hollóháza

UKRAINE

RSOD-ABAÚJ-
ZEMPLÉN

Tokaj

Miskolc　　**SZABOLCS-
SZATMÁR-BEREG**

övesd　Nyíregyháza

bágy
al Park　Debrecen

Hajdúszoboszló

HAJDÚ-BIHAR

TRANSYLVANIA

ROMANIA

KÉS

**Aggtelek National
   Park D2
Austria A4–B2**

**Bács-Kiskun (county)
   C3–D4
Bakony Mountains
   B3–C3
Balatonfüred C3
Baranya (county) B4–C5
Békés (county) D3–E4
Borsod-Abaúj-Zemplén
   (county) D1–F2
Budapest (city) C3
Budapest (municipal
   county) C3
Bükk Mountains E2**

**Carpathian Mountains
   B1–F1
Croatia A4–C5
Csongrád (county)
   D3–D4
Czech Republic A1–C1**

**Danube (river) A2–D5
Debrecen E3**

Eger D2

**Fejér (county) C3
Fertőd B3**

**Great Alföld D3–D4
Gyöngyös D2
Győr-Moson-Sopron
   (county) B2–B3**

**Hajdú-Bihar (county)
   E2–E3
Hajdúszoboszló E3
Herend B3
Heves (county) D2–E2
Hévíz B3
Hódmezővásárhely D4
Hollóháza E1
Hortobágy National
   Park E3**

**Jász-Nagykun-Szolnok
   (county) D2–E3**

**Kalocsa C4
Kiskunhalas D4
Komárom-Esztergom
   (county) C2–C3**

**Lake Balaton B4–C3
Little Alföld B3–C3**

**Mátra Mountains C2–D2
Mezőkövesd D2
Miskolc E2
Mohács C4
Mount Kékes D2**

**Nógrád (county) C2–D2
Northern Mountains D2
Nyíregyháza E2**

**Pécs C4
Pest (county) C2–D3**

Romania E3–F5

**Serbia C4–E5
Slovakia B2–F1
Slovenia A3–A5
Somogy (county)
   B4–C3
Sopron B2
Szabolcs-Szatmár-Bereg
   (county) E2–F2
Szeged D4**

**Tapolca B3
Tisza (river) D5–F2
Tokaj E2
Tolna (county) C3–C4
Transdanubia (region)
   B4–C4
Transylvania (region) F3**

Ukraine F1–F2

**Vas (county) A3–B3
Veszprém (county)
   B3–C3**

Zala (county) A3–B4

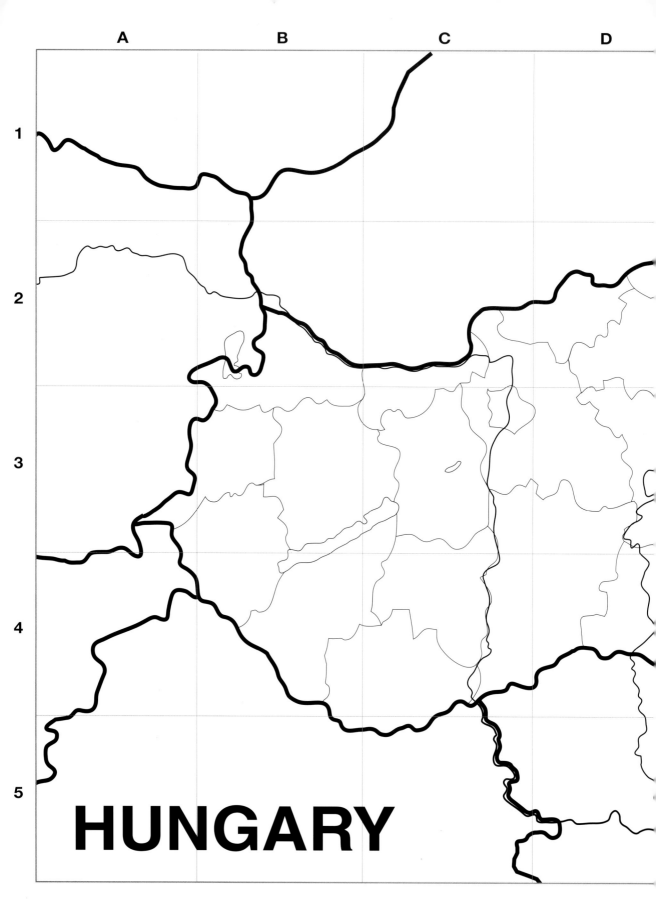

A B C D

1

2

3

4

5

HUNGARY

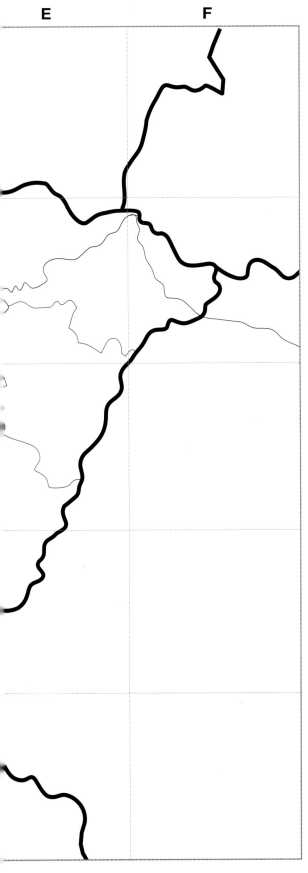

E   F

How Is Your Geography?

Learning to identify the main geographical areas and points of a country can be challenging. Although it may seem difficult at first to memorize the locations and spellings of major cities or the names of mountain ranges, rivers, deserts, lakes, and other prominent physical features, the end result of this effort can be very rewarding. Places you previously did not know existed will suddenly come to life when referred to in world news, whether in newspapers, television reports, or other books and reference sources. This knowledge will make you feel a bit closer to the rest of the world, with its fascinating variety of cultures and physical geography.

Used in a classroom setting, the instructor can make duplicates of this map using a copy machine. (PLEASE DO NOT WRITE IN THIS BOOK!) Students can then fill in any requested information on their individual map copies. Used one-on-one, the student can also make copies of the map on a copy machine and use them as a study tool. The student can practice identifying place names and geographical features on his or her own.

Hungary at a Glance

Official Name	Republic of Hungary
Capital	Budapest
Official Language	Hungarian
Population	10.1 million
Land Area	35,919 square miles (93,030 square km)
Coastline	landlocked (0 miles/0 km)
Counties	Bács-Kiskun, Baranya, Békés, Borsod-Abaúj-Zemplén, Budapest (municipal), Csongrád, Fejér, Gyõr-Moson-Sopron, Hajdú-Bihar, Heves, Jász-Nagykun-Szolnok, Komárom-Esztergom, Nógrád, Pest, Somogy, Szabolcs-Szatmár-Bereg, Tolna, Vas, Veszprém, Zala
Highest Point	Mount Kékes 3,327 feet (1,014 m)
Border Countries	Austria, Croatia, Romania, Serbia, Slovakia, Slovenia, Ukraine
Major Rivers	Danube, Tisza
Major Religions	Roman Catholic, Calvinist Protestant, Lutheran
National Anthem	*Himnusz*
Holidays	New Year (January 1)
	National Day (March 15)
	Good Friday (March/April)
	Saint Stephen's Day (August 20)
	Saint Nick's Day (December 6)
Famous Leaders	King Matthias Corvinus (1443–1490)
	Empress Maria Theresa (1717–1780)
	Lajos Kossuth (1802–1894)
Currency	Hungarian Forint (HUF 281.65 = U.S. $1 in 2001)

Opposite: **The facade of Matthias Church in Budapest is richly ornamented and intricately detailed.**

Glossary

Hungarian Words

csárda (CHAHR-daw): village inn.

Csárdás (CHAHR-dahsh): Hungary's national dance.

csikósok (CHEE-kohsh-ohk): Hungarian cowboys.

cukrászdák (TSU-crahs-dahk): pastry shops that also serve coffee.

dupla (DUE-plaw): a cup of coffee consisting of two shots of espresso.

eszpresszók (ES-press-ohk): coffeehouses that also serve alcoholic beverages.

Halas (HAW-lawsh): a distinctively Hungarian lace that is prized among collectors.

huszár (HOO-sahr): a Magyar who possesses fine horsemanship.

kávé (KAH-vay): a cup of coffee consisting of one shot of espresso, with sugar and milk on the side.

kávéház (KAH-vay-hahz): a coffeehouse.

palacsinta (PAW-law-chin-taw): stuffed crepes.

Puszta (POOS-taw): vast grasslands in the Great Hungarian Plain.

rendörség (REN-duhr-shage): police.

szálloda (SAH-low-daw): hotel.

szür (SEE-ur): a cloak.

tejeskávé (TAY-esh-kah-vay): a large cup of milky coffee.

English Vocabulary

acquaint: become familiar with.

amphitheater: a round or oval building with a central open space surrounded by rising rows of seats.

appliqués: decorations or trimmings made of one material and attached by sewing or gluing to another.

artifacts: objects made by humans for a practical purpose.

assimilate: conform to the customs or attitudes of a dominant cultural group or national culture.

canonized: declared to be an officially recognized saint.

clergies: groups of persons, such as ministers, ordained for religious service.

communism: theory or system of social organization based on common ownership of property and equality of the people.

contamination: the act of dirtying or infecting previously clean resources.

cultivation: the act of growing plants or crops from seeds, bulbs, or shoots.

customarily: according to or depending on custom; usually; habitually.

deciduous: types of trees that shed their leaves at a particular time of year.

demarcated: set or marked the limits of.

discrimination: the act of treating a person or group unfairly or with prejudice because of differences in race or ethnicity.

disrupted: disturbed or interrupted the orderly course of a given event.

dwindling: diminishing, shrinking, or becoming smaller.

elite: the group or part of society that is considered the finest, most distinguished, and most powerful.

equestrian: of or pertaining to horseback riding or horseback riders.

exodus: a mass departure or emigration.

expatriates: people who live and work away from their native country.

exploitation: the careless use of land resources, people, etc., especially for profit.

federation: a centralized union of several tribes, states, organizations, etc., each of which retains control of its own internal affairs.

glaze: a liquid mixture of sugar syrup used to form a thin, clear coating on top of foods.

hostile: unfriendly; antagonistic; not hospitable.

immense: huge; vast; seemingly immeasurable or limitless.

indiscriminate: making choices without careful consideration.

industrialization: the process of becoming a society in which the economy is characterized by major industries, machinery production, and large concentrations of workers in cities.

ingenuity: cleverness; inventiveness.

instill: impart ideas, principles, or feelings over a period of time.

institutionalized: made into a system that consists of an established set of customs or practices.

irrigation: supplying land with water by means of ditches or artificial channels.

marzipan: a colorful confection molded from a paste made of ground almonds, sugar, and egg whites.

metallurgy: the science of separating metals from their ores.

nationalism: patriotism or devotion to one's nation.

nomadic herdsmen: people who roam from one place to another for pasture while keeping or tending a herd.

nuclear families: basic social units that each consist of a father, a mother, and their children.

outskirts: the outlying regions or districts, as of a city.

pagan: not Christian, Muslim, Jewish, or of any specific, organized religion; heathen.

pharmaceuticals: legal drugs or chemicals, usually prescribed as medication.

picturesque: visually charming, as if resembling, or being a suitable subject for, a painting.

premises: a piece of property that includes both a building and its grounds.

premium: of high value or price because of scarcity.

prioritize: assign differing degrees of importance to events, objects, or circumstances.

prominent: widely and favorably known.

resilient: recovering easily and quickly from unpleasant or damaging events.

scorching: the effect of browning or killing plants by exposure to hot, relentless sunlight.

stifling: oppressive and suffocating.

symbolic: serving as a representation, or symbol, of something.

tumultuous: full of unrest and instability.

unprecedented: unheard of; never before known or experienced.

vineyards: land devoted to cultivating grapes eventually used to make wine.

More Books to Read

The Architecture of Historic Hungary. Dora Wiebenson and József Sisa, eds. (MIT Press)

Earthen Wonders: Hungarian Ceramics Today. Carolyn M. Bardos (Lake House)

Hungary. Culinaria series. Aniko Gergely, Ruprecht Stempell, and Christoph Buechel (Konemann)

Hungary. Major World Nations series. Julian Popescu (Chelsea House)

Hungary. Nations in Transition series. Raymond Hill (Facts on File)

Hungary/Budapest. The Green Guide series. Michelin Staff, ed. (Michelin Travel Publications)

Hungary: Crossroads of Europe. Exploring Cultures of the World series. Richard Steins (Benchmark Books)

Hungary in Pictures. Visual Geography series. (Lerner)

Prince of the Stable: A Hungarian Legend. Legends of the World series. Christopher Keane (Troll)

Simple Guide to Customs and Etiquette in Hungary. Simple Guides: Customs and Etiquette series. Laszlo Jotischky (Paul Norbury)

The White Stag. Kate Seredy (Econo-Clad Books)

Videos

Enemy Mine — Hungary: Where the Water Is Deep. (Mystic Fire)

Hungary: Budapest. (Education 2000)

Sir George Solti: Hungarian Connections. (Uni/London Classics)

Web Sites

www.fsz.bme.hu/hungary/homepage.html

www.hungary.org/users/hipcat/

www.kfki.hu/keptar

Due to the dynamic nature of the Internet, some web sites stay current longer than others. To find additional web sites, use a reliable search engine with one or more of the following keywords to help you locate information about Hungary. Keywords: *Csárdás, Danube, Eger,* goulash, *Hortobágy, Lake Balaton, Magyars,* Puszta, *Roma.*

Index